"La découverte d'un mets nouveau fait plus pour le bonheur du genre humain que la découverte d'une étoile."

The discovery of a new dish does more for the happiness of humankind than the discovery of a star.

Anthelme Brillat-Savarin, Physiologie du goût (1825), Aphorisme IX

Medieval Inspired Window

The Pâtissier

The Pâtissier

Recipes and Conversations
from Alsace, France

Hossine Bennara and Susan Lundquist
with Photographs by
Frederic Lacroix

iUniverse, Inc.
New York Lincoln Shanghai

The Pâtissier
Recipes and Conversations from Alsace, France

Copyright © 2006 by Susan Lundquist

iUniverse books may be ordered through booksellers or by contacting:

iUniverse
2021 Pine Lake Road, Suite 100
Lincoln, NE 68512
www.iuniverse.com
1-800-Authors (1-800-288-4677)

ISBN-13: 978-0-595-36505-0 (pbk)
ISBN-13: 978-0-595-80938-7 (ebk)
ISBN-10: 0-595-36505-1 (pbk)
ISBN-10: 0-595-80938-3 (ebk)

Printed in the United States of America

Dedicated to Sandrine Aubry and Laurent Federlin.
Thank you for your generosity, enthusiasm,
and friendship during the making of this book.

We would like to thank our families, who have provided nourishment and inspiration over the years. Our thanks to Laurent Federlin's grandparents for help translating the recipes' titles into Alsatian and including us in the experience of a traditional tarte flambée meal in your home. A special thank-you to Martine Sechoy Wolff, Jill Lundquist, Shelly Theissen, Sally Lundquist, Steve Biama, and Sarah Johnson for your support testing, editing, and providing valuable feedback in the making of this book.

Contents

Strasbourg Cathedral

Introduction

This book was born out of a chance encounter between an American spending a year in France and her neighbor, an Alsatian chef. It happened like this.

We had just moved into our new place a few days earlier. Our apartment was in the heart of the aptly named "Petite France," the oldest and most beautiful neighborhood in the city of Strasbourg in Alsace, France. The location was great! We had a view of the canals where swans frolicked all day while fishermen tried their luck. We were just ten minutes walking distance from the seemingly ageless gothic cathedral. The chiming of bells in the bell tower marked the hours of each day. The streets around us were paved with worn cobblestones that one imagined cut and polished by generations of passionate artisans. Our building was a tired eighteenth century half-timbered house of Alsatian style with crisscrossing beams of wood that somehow kept the building standing as it leaned slightly to one side. The state of the carpet, which had surely never been washed, attested to the authenticity. The plumbing conformed to the norms from Napoleon's days, and the electrical system seemed to be daring the flames to come and roast us like chickens on a spit. Exposed wiring ran along the wooden beams of the ceiling. Fuses would burst each time we tried to use the two stove plates simultaneously. In other words, it was perfect! We were in search of the authentic European life after spending a few years in Silicon Valley, and we were going to get it.

Soon, we were swimming in the "authentic life." Our first challenge was to convince the landlord to repair the toilet. This was not a simple task as the owner, Monsieur Metzger, a ninety-year-old Alsatian who had known the horrors and hardships of World War II would counter our request with "Hopla, no problem, there is a nice toilet in the hallway." After a few days of pathetic pleas and sitting on the hallway toilet with my knees pressed against the door and the toilet paper in my lap, I persuaded M. Metzger finally to give in and the "plumber" (another renter) arrived to provide us with one of life's small luxuries.

Our happiness lasted until the next morning when I woke up with large, red, itchy bumps all over my arms and hands. What was happening? Our first suspicion was the new bed sheets! Maybe they contained nongenetically modified cotton or an additive that was foreign and unknown to my skin! Hopla! I ran to the store to try to exchange the sheets, a very perilous enterprise, as customer service is about as popular a concept in France as the books of Jean-Paul Sartre are in Texas. The sales lady argued "Madame, surely you do not expect me to take back *used* sheets!" Then I showed her my ravaged arms in front of a line of customers. They looked like the arms of someone who had escaped the black plague, and she was suddenly willing to do whatever it took to get me out of the store. She handed me the money without touching my hand and I handed her the suspicious cotton.

Ouf! But the following morning, new pimples had appeared and this time they were also on my feet. Horror! What should I do? My mind raced for answers. Was it an allergic reaction to the French reality show that I watched the night before, where the participants, mostly scantily clad women, had to pretend to be farmers and shovel cow excrement around on a farm? Was there a new strain of the black plague emerging? Was I going to be the first victim? Or maybe it was the unwashed carpet, stuffed with all kinds of mysterious substances and bacteria. We went to see M. Metzger to try to convince him to change the carpeting in the apartment, still using my bloodied swollen arms as an argument. But M. Metzger was not impressed. "My dear, you have to go see a doctor; you are sick, no doubt from some bad cold. I will call my friend, the professor Maréchal, and get you a rendezvous."

The professor Maréchal, who specialized in infectious and venereal diseases (hmmm – let's not digress), received me in his cabinet and inspected my arms closely. "Madame, those are symptoms of mite bites. It is of course hard to identify the species from just the mark on the skin, but I would venture to name *Dermatophagoides pteronyssinus*, a common species of mite, as the guilty party." My skin crawled, as I remembered the videos concerning the life of eyebrow-dwelling mites I had seen in science class. Noticing my look of disgust, he quickly added, "No, Madame, no, do not be troubled, but you have not by any chance bought recently some delicious fromage from Auvergne? Mites are added to some types of cheese to enhance their flavor, and then they are sublime and fit for the palate of the greatest gourmet! So you should be thankful that they exist! But in your case, you must disinfect the apartment, wash all the clothes in boiling water, and throw out the mattress! You owe me twenty-five euros."

Hopla, that was all Frederic needed to know. I never saw him so determined to confront M. Metzger. He was strong, forceful, and above all overwhelmed by the realization that he had been sleeping with the same mites, but he had no reaction to the bites like I did. That meant that they could be all over him and he wouldn't know it! M. Metzger didn't stand a chance. He agreed to replace the mattress and carpet, and we promptly went to throw the old mattress and carpet out the window, disinfect all of our clothing, set off bug bombs and set up sleeping bags on the sterilized kitchen floor.

The neighbor, Hossine Bennara, who goes by the nickname Ben and is a native Alsatian and pastry chef, seeing our long tired faces and hearing about our troubles, had pity on us and invited us to dinner the same evening. He cooked up a very simple dinner composed of a green salad (see page 52), a flammkueche (tarte flambée, see page 51), a glass of white Riesling (see your favorite wine store), and for dessert a fabulous tarte aux pommes (see page 54), the best apple pie to ever cross my lips, a pie that tasted like the first pie baked by the first woman and eaten by the first man in the dawn of times. We devoured his pie while he looked on with surprise at our ferocity and began to tell us about his life in Alsace, memories from his village when he was small, stories about Christmas when his mother cooked traditional pastries such as Mannala, Bredele, and all the little Pains d'épices, his training as a pastry chef, his time in the army, all of that accompanied with "Another glass of Riesling? Or a piece of tart?"

That evening was the first of many. This book was born during those evenings, while hearing Ben's stories and dining at his table. The concept of the book came naturally: a collection of stories and meals reflecting his life and family recipes in Alsace. The meals use ingredients traditionally available in each season of the year in Alsace. There is one meal for each month to which is associated a little story taken from Ben's repertoire, a story that will hopefully make you smile. Alsace is a small region of France, but it has an amazingly rich gastronomy that holds its own among all the other regions of France. We hope that this book will be, as it was for us, a source of joy, companionship, and good food.

The Old Customs Office

A Brief History of Alsace, France

Alsace is a long stretch of land bordered by the Vosges Mountains to the west, Belgium and Germany to the north, the Rhine River to the east, and Switzerland to the south. Its location at the intersection of so many competing powers means that it has been invaded, pillaged, and has changed hands countless times in the course of history. This has had profound influence on the language, lifestyle, architecture, and gastronomy of the region. The official language is French, but the traditional language is a German dialect still spoken in many families, although spelling and grammar vary throughout the region. Gastronomically speaking, the substrate of the cuisine is Germanic, to which Jewish influences and French techniques and refinements have been added. The climate is hot and sunny in summer, which suits itself to the cultivation of the vine. Alsace's claims to fame include the invention of the "pâté de foie gras," the kougelhopf, the Christmas tree, "Christkindelsmaerik," or outdoor markets during Christmas time, and world famous white wines and late-harvest wines. It is the home of the European parliament, boasts one of the most important densities of three-star Michelin restaurants in France, and finally, it is the home of historic cities such as Strasbourg and Colmar that have preserved medieval architecture.

To keep track of the history of the region is no small feat, so we have prepared a short résumé of the principal important historical and culinary events that have marked the region. Human presence in the area goes back to at least 600,000 BC, stone tools having been found on many prehistorical sites. However, recorded history only really begins with the Roman conquest.

1500 BC	Invasion of Celtic tribes from the east.
58 BC	Roman invasion. Julius Cesar defeats the German chieftain Arioviste. Camps and forts are built along the Rhine River to protect the colonies from the "barbarians." The camp named Argentoratum will become Strasbourg. The integration of Alsace into the Roman Empire means that the region was economically and culturally linked to the regions across the Empire. The Romans brought many plants, spices, and vegetables with them, some of them originally from the Middle East and India, some varieties of grapevine, cabbage, celery, cucumber, parsley, anis, and cumin. Jewish settlers most likely established in the region at this time. The largest and most important Jewish community was located in Alsace up to World War II.
AD 235	Invasion of the Alamans, a German tribe (note that "Allemand" still remains the word for German in French). The Romans abandon the region. The Alamans are the origin of the Alsatian dialect, which endures to this day.
343	First Christian bishop in Strasbourg. Christianity establishes itself in the area.

496   Defeat of the Alamans at the hands of the Francs (another German tribe). Francs control a great deal of what is now France (hence the name!).

742–814   Charlemagne's rule. The first Christmas tree is mentioned in connection with the emperor's visit to Sélestat, a village in Alsace. It is said they decorated a tree in honor of his visit at Christmas time and continued the tradition in commemoration. Strasbourg is known as the Christmas "capital" of the world. The city is brilliantly decorated and open-air markets abound during that time.

870   Alsace is integrated into the Holy Roman Empire (which covers much of the territory of modern day Germany). Ginger is imported into Europe from India. Saffron is introduced into Spain by the Arabs and passes into France.

1349   The Black Plague. Roughly twenty-five percent of the population of Europe dies. Jews, presumed guilty by default, are put to death and banished from the cities. Cereal and vegetable porridges constitute the base of daily peasant food, sometimes with some pork or pork fat. Jews use goose fat instead of pork fat and incorporate geese into the cuisine.

1350   Irish monks in Alsace invent Munster cheese.

1434   Johannes Gensfleisch, called Gutenberg, lives in Strasbourg just before inventing the printing press in Mainz.

1517   Luther preaches the reform. It takes root solidly in Alsace. Preachers denounce the excesses of some that conduct feasts, even going as far as using the altar in the cathedral as a table to hold the food! Later, laws limit the number of guests (maximum 12 in some cities), duration (maximum of two days!), and number of courses of festive occasions such as weddings.

1618–1648   Thirty Years' War: Alsace is ravaged. The treaty of Westphalia brings Alsace into the kingdom of France. French governors and officers bring their cooks, who introduce French techniques into local cuisine. Forks appear. Average daily consumption of wine is estimated to be 1.5 liters per person (for the merchant class, not for the peasants!). The potato, originally from South America, is introduced. Sugar is also introduced.

1671   Abbé Buchinger first mentions spaetzles in a cookbook. However, the recipe was known to the Romans.

1693   Jakob Amman brings to life the Amish movement in Sainte-Marie-aux-Mines in Alsace.

1750   Coffee and chocolate appear in Strasbourg.

1780   Inspired by a Jewish recipe, Jean-Pierre Clause, chef of the Maréchal de Contades, invents the "pâté de foie gras en croûte" in Strasbourg. However, the ancient Egyptians who noticed that migrating geese fed more than usual before taking flight probably discovered the first foie gras.

1789   French Revolution.

1791	The revolution proclaims the equality of rights for all citizens, including the Jews of Alsace (50,000 Jews in Alsace compared to only 5,000 in Paris).
1792	Rouget de l'Isle composes, "La Marseillaise," in the city of Strasbourg.
1834	Frédéric Auguste Bartholdi, creator of the statue of Liberty, is born.
1871	Franco-German War. Alsace becomes part of the German Reich. The vines are neglected in place of beer. Many breweries are established.
1873	Asparagus, imported from Algeria by Pastor Heyler, is planted for the first time in Hoerdt, Alsace.
1800-1900	The economy grows and the daily food and fare gets better. Travelers throughout Alsace remark on how much food is eaten here. An estimated 134kg of meat is consumed annually per person in Strasbourg.
1918	After World War I, Alsace returns to France. The neglected vines are renewed and enjoy much esteem. The breweries, however, are not neglected. Both beer and wine is produced in the region, which is unique. Alsace continues to be the main beer producer of France, including such breweries as Kronenbourg, Heineken, and Fischer.
1940	Alsace is integrated into the Third Reich. Tens of thousands of young Alsatians are enrolled by force into the Wehrmacht and sent to the Russian front. Many do not return home.
1944	American and Allied forces liberate Alsace from German occupation. Alsace is reunited with France once again.
1945	The Counsel of Europe is established in Strasbourg.
Today	No other change of allegiance in sight! The European Parliament is in Strasbourg.

Bibliography
Jean-Paul Grasser, "*Une histoire de l'Alsace,*" Editions Jean-Paul Gisserot, 1988, 123 pp.
Jean-Louis Schlienger, André Braun, "*Le mangeur alsacien,*" La Nuée Bleue, 2000, 285 pp.

The Wines of Alsace

Gastronomical Festivals of Alsace

Month	Festival	Specialty	City
April	Fête des Escargots	Snails	Osenbach
May	Fête de la Carpe Frite	Fried Carp	Friesen
	Fête des Asperges	Asparagus	Village-Neuf
June	Fête du Kougelhopf	Kougelhopf	Ribeauvile
	Fête du Marcassin	Wild Boar	Hattstatt
	Fête du Fromage Blanc	Cream Cheese	Orbey
	Fête de la Friture	Fried Food	Illhaeusern
	Fête de la Cerise	Cherries	Westhoffen
July	Fête du Pate en Croute	Pate Pie	Marckolsheim
	Fête du Pinot Noir	Pinot Noir Wine	Rodern
August	Fête des Amandes	Almonds	Mittelwihr
	Fête du Vin	Wine	Colmar
	Fête du Coquelet	Cockerel Chicken	Geispolsheim
	Fête du Pain d'épices	Spiced Breads	Gertwiller
	Fête du Reisling	Reisling Wine	Riquewihr
September	Fête de la Choucroute	Sauerkraut	Colmar
	Fête de la Carpe Frite	Fried Carp	Didenheim
	Fête de la Bière	Beer	Hochfelden
	Fête de la Planchette Paysanne	Country Food	Plobsheim
October	Fête des Noix	Walnuts	Geispolsheim
	Fête de la Tourte	Meat Pie	Munster
	Fête du Vin Bourru	Young Wine	Obernai
December	Marché de Noël	Christmas Market	Strasbourg

Epicerie, Some people still like their markets and stores small

Substitutions and Shortcuts

Alsatian Ingredients	US Ingredients
Balsamic vinegar	Xeres vinegar or red wine vinegar
Boudin blanc sausages	Any mild sausage
Calvados	Apple or other fruit brandy
Cervelas sausages	Any cooked bologna-style sausage
Crème de Cassis	Blueberry juice
Crème fraîche	Mix 1 C. sour cream with 1 C. heavy whipping cream
	Or, 1 C. sour cream with 1/4 C. half and half
Damson plums	Prunes
Dandelion leaves	Radicchio or other bitter lettuce leaf
Deer meat	Beef or lamb
Emmental cheese	Swiss cheese
Endive lettuce	Radicchio or other bitter lettuce leaf
Escargot	Mushrooms, shrimp, or scallops
Fresh Munster cheese	Ricotta cheese, cream cheese, or strained fromage blanc
Frog legs	Chicken breast, calamari, shrimp, or mushrooms
Fromage blanc	Mix 1 C. ricotta cheese with 1 tbs. yogurt and a pinch of salt.
	Or, 1 C. cream cheese with 1/3 C. heavy cream or plain yogurt and a pinch of salt.
Gewürztraminer or Riesling	Any sweet white wine
Goose	Duck, turkey, or chicken
Goose fat	Duck fat or butter
Guinea hen	Chicken, Cornish game hen
Herbs de Provence	A mixture of thyme, rosemary, savory, marjoram, and oregano
Honey and herb vinegar (Melfor)	Champagne vinegar or white wine vinegar
Kirsch (cherry brandy)	Any nonsugared fruit brandy or eau de vie
Knacks	Hotdogs
Lamb	Beef or pork roast
Madeira	Tawny port
Marc de Gewürztraminer	Grappa, schnapps, or cognac
Mirabelle plums	Small plums, cherries, or apricots
Munster cheese	Pecorino, tome, or other aged cheese
Pike fish	Trout or other freshwater fish

Alsatian Ingredients	US Ingredients
Pinot Noir	Any burgundy or fruity red wine
Poire Williams schnapps	Pear or other fruit brandy
Puff pastry	Premade puff pastry dough or piecrust dough
Quail eggs	Chicken eggs
Rabbit	Chicken
Red and black lumpfish eggs	Caviar or salmon eggs
Schnapps	Fruit brandy or any strong distilled alcohol
Short crust pastry	Premade piecrust dough
Spatzele	Egg pasta
Star anise	Licorice root
Strasbourg sausages	Bratwurst sausages
Tarte flambée dough	Pizza dough
Tokay Pinot Gris or Sylvaner	Sauvignon blanc or dry white wine
Truffles	Black chanterelle mushrooms
Vin bourru	Grape juice, fresh apple cider, or hard cider

General Recipes

Saturday Morning Market

Alsatian Vinaigrette

"Vinaigrette"
Vinaigrette Alsacienne

Alsace produces traditional white wine vinegar, containing a bit of honey and infused with herbs and plants, called "Melfort." If you can find it, try it with this recipe, or make your own!

Preparation: 2 minutes

2 tbs. honey and herb vinegar
1/2 tbs. Dijon mustard
Splash of Worcestershire sauce
Pinch of salt
Pinch of pepper
3 tbs. olive oil

1. Whisk vinegar, mustard, Worcestershire sauce, salt, and pepper in bowl.
2. Continue to whisk while slowly adding the olive oil.

Tips and Suggestions:
If the honey and herb vinegar is not available, champagne vinegar or white wine vinegar may be substituted.

Curried Vinaigrette

"Curry Vinaigrette"
Vinaigrette au curry

Preparation: 2 minutes

3 tbs. honey and herb vinegar
1/2 tbs. parsley
1 tsp. curry powder
1/4 tsp. sugar
1/4 tsp. salt
Pinch of pepper
2 tbs. olive oil
1 tbs. cream

1. Whisk vinegar and spices together.
2. Slowly add the oils and then cream while whisking.

Tips and suggestions:
Champagne vinegar or white wine vinegar may be substituted for the honey and herb vinegar.
Walnut or peanut oil may be substituted for the hazelnut oil.

Nutmeg Vinaigrette

"Muscadenouss"
Vinaigrette aux noix de muscade

Preparation: 2 minutes

2 tbs. honey and herb vinegar
1/8 tsp. nutmeg
Pinch of salt
Pinch of pepper
Pinch of sugar
3 tbs. walnut oil

1.   Whisk vinegar and spices together.
2.   Slowly add the walnut oil while whisking.

Tips and suggestions:
Champagne vinegar or white wine vinegar may be substituted for the honey and herb vinegar.

Dijon Vinaigrette

"Senf vinaigrette"
Vinaigrette à la moutarde de Dijon

Preparation: 2 minutes

2 tbs. honey and herb vinegar
1 tbs. Dijon mustard
1/2 tsp. thyme
Pinch of salt
Pinch of pepper
Pinch of sugar
3 tbs. olive oil

1.   Whisk vinegar, mustard, and spices together.
2.   Slowly add the olive oil while whisking.

Tips and suggestions:
Tarragon may be substituted for thyme.
Champagne vinegar or white wine vinegar may be substituted for the honey and herb vinegar.

Balsamic Vinaigrette

"Balsamique vinaigrette"

Vinaigrette balsamique

Preparation: 2 minutes

2 tbs. balsamic vinegar
Pinch of salt
Pinch of pepper
Pinch of sugar
3 tbs. olive oil

1. Whisk vinegar and spices together.
2. Slowly add the olive oil while whisking.

Tips and suggestions:
Xeres or red wine vinegar may be substituted for the balsamic vinegar.
A pinch of thyme or basil may be added according to taste.

Mayonnaise

"Mayonnaise"

Preparation: 5 minutes

3 egg yolks
1/8 tsp. white wine vinegar
Pinch of salt
Pinch of pepper
3/4 C. olive oil
Minced garlic clove
Pinch of parsley

1. Whisk egg yolks and vinegar in a bowl until light yellow and creamy. Add salt and pepper.
2. Continue to whisk while slowly adding olive oil.
3. Stir in garlic and parsley and refrigerate.

Tips and suggestions:
If you are worried about raw eggs, use organic eggs. They are generally safer.
Ready-made mayonnaise may also be used with the garlic and parsley added to taste.

Horseradish Sauce

"Merettichsoss"
Sauce au raifort

In Alsace, horseradish has been an important condiment for salads, cold meats, and sausages since the Middle Ages, perhaps because it could disguise the taste of not-so-fresh meat. Each fall, families were sure to stock enough horseradish and mustard to last through the winter.

Preparation: 10 minutes

1/2 C. horseradish
1 C. warm water
1/2 C. breadcrumbs
1/4 C. milk
Pinch of sugar
1 tbs. vinegar
1 tsp. mustard
1/4 C. crème fraîche
1/8 tsp. salt

1. Finely grate the horseradish and soak in the warm water until it expands. Drain excess liquid.
2. Soak breadcrumbs in the milk and drain. Add sugar, vinegar, and mustard to horseradish and mix well.
3. Add the crème fraîche and salt to taste.

Tips and suggestions:
To save time, you can buy a prepared horseradish sauce and add a little crème fraîche.
Sour cream may be substituted for the crème fraîche.
Note: Crème fraîche recipe is available in this book if not available to you locally.

Mousseline Sauce

"Musselinesoss"
Sauce mousseline

This sauce is traditionally served as one of the three sauces in "Asperges aux trois sauces" (three sauce asparagus), a traditional dish available during asparagus season (around the beginning of May).

Preparation: 10 minutes

1/4 C. butter
1/4 C. flour
2 C. chicken broth
2 egg yolks
1/4 C. crème fraîche
Juice of 1 lemon
Pinch of salt
Pinch of pepper
Pinch of nutmeg
Fresh tarragon

1. Melt the butter in a saucepan over medium heat. Add flour and stir until golden. Lower heat and add chicken broth and stir until sauce thickens.
2. Whisk 2 egg yolks with crème fraîche and add lemon juice, salt, pepper, and nutmeg.
3. Add the hot chicken broth mixture slowly to the egg yolk mixture while whisking constantly. Return to stove and cook over low heat while stirring constantly until thick.

Tips and suggestions:
It is best to serve this sauce immediately. If you want to make it in advance, refrigerate it and warm it slightly before serving.
Fresh chives may be substituted for the tarragon. Sour cream may be substituted for the crème fraîche.
Note: Crème fraîche recipe is in this book if not available to you locally.

Crème Fraîche

"Frescher Rahm"
Crème fraîche

It is nearly impossible to complete an Alsatian menu without crème fraîche as an ingredient. Crème fraîche is a dairy culture that resembles a light sour cream. It is appearing on more and more grocery store shelves in the US, but if not available, it is easy to make yourself.

Preparation: 5 minutes

3 C. heavy cream
1 C. plain yogurt or buttermilk.

1. Mix cream and yogurt in a bowl.
2. Cover with a towel and set in a warm place for 12 hours until the cream thickens. Refrigerate.

Tips and suggestions:
This keeps in the refrigerator for up to 2 weeks.

Fresh Cream Cheese

"Bibbeleskäs"
Fromage Blanc

This is also sometimes called "fresh Munster cheese." It is similar to a ricotta cheese or a soft cream cheese. It is available in some stores under the French name of "fromage blanc."

Preparation: 10 minutes

1 liter fresh warm milk
1 tbs. rennet

Cheesecloth

1. Mix the milk and rennet, and let it curdle for 1 hour. Strain through cheesecloth for 1 hour.
2. Place in a wooden bowl or pine mold using the cheesecloth as a lining and refrigerate overnight.

Frying Batter

"Kücheteig"
Pâte à frire

This is a batter used to coat food before frying in hot oil. For desserts, add a teaspoon of sugar and a pinch of cinnamon to the batter.

Preparation: 5 minutes

Culture: 1 hour

1 C. flour
1/2 tsp. salt
2 tbs. vegetable oil
1 C. beer
1/2 tsp. vinegar
2 egg whites

1. Mix flour, salt, oil, and beer in a bowl and stir until mixed. Add more beer if necessary. Do not overstir. The batter should coat your finger like molasses.
2. Cover with a towel and place in a warm area to rise for 1 to 2 hours.
3. Before using, beat the egg whites with vinegar until firm and fold gently into the batter. Fry in oil at 300°F.

Tips and suggestions:
Before coating your food, drop a bit of the batter into your oil to be sure that it is at a proper temperature. It should sizzle and turn golden in about 1 minute.

Tarte Flambée Dough

"Matzeteig"

Pâte à tarte flambée

A friend's grandmother made this for me for a birthday dinner in which tartes flambées were served. Some of her advice included using three different kinds of flour and keeping the breadboard full of flour when rolling out the dough so that it slides into the oven easily.

Preparation: 15 minutes
For 1 Tarte flambée:

1 C. flour
Pinch of salt
Water

1. Place the flour in a bowl and mix in the salt. Form a hole in the center and pour in a little water.

2. Mix with your hands, adding water until the flour forms into bread dough. It shouldn't be too sticky.

3. Shape into a ball and place on a floured breadboard. Roll into a rectangle. The dough should be very thin, about 1/8"–1/4" so that it bakes quickly. Keep the board well floured so that it can easily slide into the oven or onto the baking sheet.

Tips and suggestions:

The traditional cooking method is to deposit the tarte flambée on the bottom of a thick metal or stone oven in which a fire has been previously lit. The glowing embers are cleared to make room for the tarte flambée. The intense heat cooks the dough nicely in a few minutes. A hot outdoor grill should give it a nice smoky flavor as well, but a kitchen oven may also be used.

Short Crust Pastry

"Butterteig"
Pâte brisée

This is a classic flaky piecrust recipe. It is used for tarts and tortes throughout Alsace.

Preparation: 5 minutes

1¾ C. flour
1/2 tsp. salt
1 tbs. sugar
1 C. cold, unsalted butter
1/3 C. cold water

1. Mix flour, salt, and sugar in a bowl. Cut butter into cubes and mix into the flour with your fingers, breaking the butter into smaller and smaller pieces until the mixture is crumbly. Do not let the butter melt.

2. Add the cold water until the mixture holds together and shape into a ball. Wrap in a towel and set in refrigerator for 1 to 2 hours before using.

Tips and suggestions:
Do not knead the dough or let the butter melt or it will become tough instead of flaky.

Puff Pastry

"Blaeterteig"
Pâte feuillettée

This is a recipe for the dough used to make France's famous croissants. It is also used for tarts and torts, as well as numerous types of pastries. The key is to layer solid butter (not melted) between layers of dough. When the butter melts, fluffy layers of pastry remain.

Preparation: 1½ hours

2 C. flour
1 tsp. salt
1⅓ C. cold,
unsalted butter
2 C. cold water

1. Mix flour and salt in a bowl. Cut 1 C. of butter into cubes and mix into the flour with your fingers, breaking the butter into smaller and smaller pieces until the mixture is crumbly. Do not let the butter melt.

2. Add cold water until the mixture forms a ball. Wrap in a towel and cool in the refrigerator for 1/2 hour. The pastry should be about the consistency of the cold butter.

3. Cut the rest of the butter in thin slices and keep cool. Roll the dough on a cold floured surface into a large square about 1/2" thick. Place the butter slices in the center and fold 4 edges of the pastry over to completely cover the butter.

4. Roll the dough into a rectangle 2 times as long as wide and fold the 2 furthest edges in like a wallet to achieve the square shape again. Roll pastry again in the other direction, folding in the other edges in the same fashion. Refrigerate for 20 minutes.

5. Repeat step 4 two more times. (The pastry should have been rolled into a rectangle and folded 6 times.)

6. Refrigerate the pastry until ready to use.

Tips and suggestions:
This dough will rise better if it is baked in a hot oven, 400° to 450 °F, at least until the crust begins to turn golden. A cold marble rolling board is useful when rolling out the dough, because it remains cool and helps to keep the butter from melting.

Cherry Schnapps Lemonade

"Kirsch limonade"
Limonade au kirsch

Kirsch is a cherry brandy traditional to Alsace. It is quite strong and delicious.

Preparation: 10 minutes
Marinating: 1 day

1 C. cherries
1/2 C. kirsch (cherry schnapps)
Juice of 2 lemons
1/4 C. sugar
1 liter of water
1 tsp. vanilla
Fresh mint leaves
Lemon slices

Tips and suggestions:
Vodka, brandy, or cassis may be substituted for kirsch.
Raspberries may be substituted for cherries.

1. Marinate cherries in schnapps 1 to 3 days.
2. Mix lemon juice, sugar and water until all the sugar is dissolved. Stir in vanilla, cherries, and schnapps.
3. Garnish with mint leaves and lemon slices. Serve cold.

Alsatian Kir Royal

"Kir met Elsässer Crémant"
Kir royal au crémant d'Alsace

Since the use of the name "champagne" is restricted by French Legislation to bubbly wines produced in the region of Champagne, "crémant" is the name used for "champagnes" produced using the "méthode champenoise" in other regions of France. Some crémants can rival good quality champagnes.

Preparation: 5 minutes

1 tbs. Marc de Gewürztraminer
5 tbs. crème de cassis
(black currant)
1 bottle crémant (champagne)
Black currant berries to garnish

1. Mix the Marc de Gewürztraminer and crème de cassis. Pour a tablespoon of cassis mixture in each champagne glass and fill the rest with champagne.

Tips and suggestions:
White or red wine may be substituted for the sparkling wine. Grappa or brandy may be substituted for the sparkling wine.

Mulled Orange Wine

"Orange warmer win"
Vin chaud aux oranges

Mulled wine is sold in outdoor stalls at the Marché de Noël in winter. It warms Christmas shoppers as they visit the kiosks looking for the perfect gift. There are many variations. White wine variations even exist. Here is a typical recipe for the "vin chaud" that can be found in the stalls in Strasbourg during the Marché de Noël in December.

Preparation: 5 minutes
Cooking: 1/2 hour

1 bottle red wine
2 oranges peeled and chopped
1/4 C. sugar
1 tbs. star anise
1 tbs. fennel seeds
3 cinnamon sticks

1. Mix all the ingredients in a saucepan. Cover and let simmer over low heat for 1/2 hour.
2. Strain and serve warm.

Tips and suggestions:
This may be made the day before and reheated before serving. If made a day before, wait to strain the spices until you are ready to serve. Note that the wine need not be of optimal quality, an average table wine will do just fine.

Mulled Raspberry Wine

"Hembeere warmer win"
Vin chaud au vinaigre de framboise

Preparation: 5 minutes
Cooking: 1/2 hour

1 bottle red wine
1 C. raspberries
1 tbs. red wine vinegar
1 tbs. crème de Cassis
2 cinnamon sticks
1 tsp. vanilla
2-3 tbs. sugar to taste
1/2 C. Perrier

1. Mix all the ingredients in a saucepan. Cover and simmer for 1/2 hour.
2. Add Perrier or any type of carbonated mineral water before serving.

Tips and suggestions:
The raspberries may be frozen or fresh for this recipe. The wine need not be of optimal quality; an average table wine will do just fine.
This may be made the day before and reheated before serving. If made a day before, wait to strain the spices until you are ready to serve.

Mulled Wine with Schnapps

"Warmer win met schnaps"
Vin chaud au schnaps

Preparation: 5 minutes
Cooking: 1/2 hour

1 bottle red wine
3 tbs. sugar
1/2 tsp. nutmeg
1 cinnamon stick
1 apple, peeled and sliced
2 cloves
1 vanilla bean
1/2 C. schnapps

1. Mix wine, sugar, nutmeg, and cinnamon in a pot. Poke cloves into pieces of the apple and add to the pot. Slice vanilla bean in half, lengthwise, and add to the pot. Cover and simmer for 30 minutes.
2. Strain the wine and pour into a serving bowl. At the table, pour schnapps into a ladle, light with a flame, and pour directly into the mulled wine. Serve with dessert.

Tips and suggestions:
You may substitute apple cider or vin bourru for this if you like.
Brandy or Calvados may be used in place of the schnapps. Create your own variation!

Saint John's Walnut Liquor

"Nussewyn"
Liqueur de noix

This liquor originates in Butten, Alsace, where it is still produced. Many families make their own, harvesting green walnuts on St. John's Day, June 24, while the walnut shells are still soft. It reminds one of a spiced port and may be served as an aperitif or digestive.

Preparation time: 10 minutes
Marinating time: 2 months

For 2 bottles:

24 green walnuts
Zest of 1 lemon
3 cloves
1 cinnamon stick
3 C. sugar
2 C. schnapps
4 C. Pinot Noir

1. Quarter the walnuts. Mix everything in a large fermenting jar and let steep for 40 days. Shake the bottle from time to time.

2. Filter and pour into separate bottles. Store in a cool place for at least another 20 days before serving.

Coffee with Cherry Schnapps

"Café met Kirschwasser"
Café à l'eau-de-vie de cerises

After a large meal, it is a tradition in Alsace to drink a shot of schnapps to aid digestion. One truly has the feeling that it melts the fats as it descends into the stomach, although this might be illusion. Kirsch is schnapps made from cherries and is the most famous of Alsatian schnapps, although many other fruits are used as well.

Preparation: 10 minutes

1 pot of coffee
6 shots of kirsch

1. Chill schnapps in refrigerator during the meal at least 1 hour.
2. Prepare coffee.
3. Pour coffee into mugs. Pour the chilled kirsch into shot glasses and serve side by side.

Tips and suggestions:
You may use any eau-de-vie or nonsugared fruit brandies in place of the kirsch. A cognac or armagnac make a nice substitution as well. Don't make the mistake of using the sugary schnapps that are readily found in the USA. Alsatian schnapps are unsweetened.

Coffee with Schnapps

"Caféschnaps"
Café à l'eau-de-vie

Preparation: 10 minutes

Fresh brewed coffee
6 shots half and half
1 tsp. sugar
6 shots of schnapps

1. Gently heat the half and half with sugar until the sugar is dissolved.
2. Serve coffee with a shot of the half and half and a shot of schnapps alongside.

Tips and suggestions:
Any eau-de-vie or fruit brandy may replace the schnapps.

Alsatian Four Spices

Quatre-épices Alsacien

Although you can find this in the grocery stores in Alsace, many households prepare their own family recipe of "Four Spices." There are numerous variations but the main spices remain as listed below.

Preparation: 2 minutes

1 tbs. ground pepper
1½ tbs. ground nutmeg
2 tsp. ground cloves
1½ tsp. powdered ginger

Some variations include adding one of the following:

1.   Mix the spices and store in a spice jar until needed.

3/4 tsp. cayenne pepper
3/4 tsp. juniper berry powder
3/4 tsp. cinnamon.

Bastille Day

January

Lumpfish Toasts

Escargot Bouchées

Salmon with Sorrel Cream Sauce

Boudin Blanc Sausages with Black Truffle Sauce and Baked Apples

Pinot Noir Goose with Vegetable Farandole

Spiced Pear Bread

Cherry Schnapps with Fresh Munster Cream Cheese

Onion Soup

Bitter Herrings

Wine Suggestions
Appetizers—Alsatian Kir Royal or Champagne
Meal—Pinot Noir or Bordeaux
Dessert— Mulled Raspberry Wine

New Year's Love

"Die Lieb isch vergaenglich, de Durscht isch laeweslaenglich."
  Love passes, thirst endures.
"D'recht Lieb nur durich de Mawe geth"
  Real love goes through the stomach.

Frederic is pacing the floor. I think he's going crazy from the aroma swirling around the apartment. The goose is almost ready and it smells delicious. How Ben managed to fit it into the tiny oven is a mystery, but he did it, and we're ready to celebrate New Year's Eve in our new apartment with our new neighbor and friend, Ben.

Ben has been showing me some of his family recipes over the past week as we prepared to celebrate the coming year in the Alsatian spirit, which is by having a decadent meal and then shooting off fireworks from any balcony or space one can find left in the crowded streets below. No one is asleep in Strasbourg tonight. We are all full of cheer and mulled wine; however, I have caught a glimpse of melancholy cloud Ben's face from time to time. He has been making comments occasionally about how lucky Frederic and I are that we both like to eat. I'm not sure how to take such a compliment, but we're in France, and I figure that there must be some cultural gap. I was not to understand the full meaning of his comment until we made our way through the meal, survived the fireworks shot off from every angle imaginable, and returned to partake of the hangover cure of creamed herrings and onion soup. This was, after all, a well-planned meal.

As it turned out, for Ben, New Year's Eve is a time woven with memories of his first love and his first heartbreak. Oh, let's call her Julie. She was a girl from the neighboring village whose mother sang in the same choral society as Ben's. As all good village mothers do, they met regularly for coffee and gossip and sometimes brought along their kids. That is how Ben met Julie and fell in love. She was marvelous, he was marvelous, they were marvelous. New love starts the same everywhere, and they were soon strolling hand in hand for hours, gazing into each other's eyes. Their courtship was practically perfect, but inevitably Ben found a flaw in Julie—she only ate thin, clear soup. Soup without crème fraîche! She had a pitiful appetite. This flaw, although minor to most people, needled Ben. But there was more to come. She started to make strange remarks such as "Ben, that's enough bacon in your salad!" or "No, Ben, stop putting cream on your quiche." No, this was not a good development.

As Ben pondered the meaning of all of this, the New Year was coming. Ben had agreed to cook for his family celebration, and he was creating new recipes to celebrate New Year's Day. New Year's Eve, however, was reserved for him and Julie. He invited Julie to his place for a romantic evening sampling the new recipes. She barely ate a thing! But after the meal, one thing led to another—after which, Ben had the munchies. Naturally, he got up and went to find some Bredele (small cakes), and then he heard Julie's voice from the bedroom. "What! You're hungry? You want to eat more? You're going to get fat if you continue like that! Look at Pierce Brosnan, he doesn't eat all the time!" There it was. The mood was spoiled. He had had enough of her soup. He replied, "Look, I'm a pâtissier! I love to eat and I love to drink wine! You don't understand. God speaks to me through bacon. The way to the heart is through the stomach! I love to put a little crème fraîche with my bacon and sauté them slowly in a frying pan and pair them with baked potatoes and a fine Riesling, hmmm…" His thoughts started to wander in fields of crisp baked potatoes. When he came to his senses again, she was gone. Ben realized that it was inevitable, and he turned to his oven for comfort. "Chefs are so misunderstood," he thought to himself. That night he would go to the New Year's fireworks with his Bredele instead of Julie, but surprisingly, it was still romantic.

Seduction and Indifference

Escargot Bouchées

"Schnecke Pastetle"

Bouchées à l'escargot

Escargot production in Alsace is now being delocalized to lower-wage countries in Eastern Europe. Is nothing sacred?!

Preparation: 15 minutes

Baking: 1/2 hour

Puff pastry (see recipe)
Glass of water
1/2 C. butter
1/4 tsp. salt
1/4 tsp. pepper
1 tsp. garlic, mashed
1 tsp. parsley, chopped
12 escargots, cleaned and precooked

1. Preheat oven to 400°F.
2. Cut puff pastry into 36 two-inch disks with a cookie cutter or a glass. In 24 of the disks cut a hole the center with a cookie cutter the size of an inch to make a donut shape.
3. Brush water on the surface of a solid disk and lay donut-shaped disk on top; brush again and layer a second donut-shaped disk to make a small tower.
4. Place all the towers on a baking sheet lined with wax paper and bake in the oven for 15 minutes until they puff up and turn slightly golden. Watch to keep from burning. Remove from oven and cool.
5. Mix the butter, salt, pepper, garlic, and parsley. Place an escargot in each tower and cover with the butter mixture.
6. Reduce temperature in oven to 350°F and bake for another 10 minutes.
7. Serve hot.

Tips and suggestions:

Mushrooms, shrimp, or scallops may be substituted for the escargot.

The escargots may be purchased cleaned and precooked.

Lumpfish Toasts

Petits toasts aux œufs de lompes

Preparation: 10 minutes

1/2 tomato
1/4 tsp. olive oil
6 slices of white bread, toasted
2 tbs. softened butter
6 tbs. red lumpfish eggs
6 tbs. black lumpfish eggs
2 lemon wedges
12 mini asparagus tips

1. Peel and seed the tomato. Mash or puree the pulp with olive oil.
2. Toast the bread and cut off the crusts. Butter and cut into triangles.
3. Spread a tablespoon of red lumpfish eggs on 6 pieces of toast and a tablespoon of black lumpfish eggs on the other 6 pieces of toast. Squeeze lemon wedges over the eggs to season. Place an asparagus tip on top of the eggs and garnish with tomato puree.
4. Serve fresh.

Tips and suggestions:
Caviar or salmon eggs may replace the lumpfish eggs.

Salmon with Sorrel Cream Sauce

"Saumon met Surampfercreme"
Saumon à la crème d'oseilles

Salmon is a festive addition to any meal. In Alsace, it can serve as the water symbol for the traditional air, water, and earth trilogy in holiday meals. Salmon and other fish are plentiful there, and sorrel is a classic herb to pair with fish.

Preparation: 15 minutes
Baking: 20 min.

Butter
1 2-lb. fresh salmon gutted and skinned (leave the head if you like)
Salt and pepper
1/4 C. lemon juice

Sauce:
1 C. sorrel leaves, chopped
1/3 C. crème fraîche (pg. X)
1/2 tsp. herbes de Provence
1 tbs. lemon juice
1 tbs. butter
1/2 tsp. salt
1/2 tsp. pepper

1. Preheat oven to 350°F.
2. Butter a ceramic baking dish. Salt and pepper both sides of the salmon. Place in baking dish and pour 1/4 cup of lemon juice over the salmon. Bake in oven for 20 minutes.
3. Prepare sorrel sauce. Place sorrel leaves, crème fraîche, herbes de Provence, lemon juice, butter, salt, and pepper in small pan. Heat gently for 10 minutes, stirring occasionally.
4. Slice salmon at the table to serve and garnish with sorrel sauce.

Tips and suggestions:
Herbes de Provence is generally a mixture of the following herbs: thyme, rosemary, savory, marjoram, and oregano.

Boudin Blanc Sausages with Black Truffle Sauce and Baked Apples

"Wissi Bleutwurst"

Boudin blanc aux truffes et pommes confites

Boudin blanc is a mild sausage composed of pork meat, bread, milk, onions, and spices and is not to be confused with boudin noir, which is mostly made up of pork meat and pork blood.

Preparation: 15 minutes
Baking: 20 minutes

1/4 C. butter
6 boudin blanc sausages
1/4 tsp. salt
1/8 tsp. pepper
1/2 tsp. shallots, minced
1 tbs. black truffles,
diced or sliced
1/2 tsp. balsamic vinegar
2 tbs. crème fraîche (pg. X)

6 small golden apples
3 tbs. honey
3 tbs. Calvados
1 tbs. water
1/2 tbs. butter

1. Melt 1/4 C. butter in frying pan and sautee the boudin blanc over high heat. Remove the boudin blanc and sauté the salt, pepper, shallots, and truffles in the remaining butter until the shallots are transparent. Deglaze with vinegar and stir in the crème fraîche. Keep warm over low heat until needed.

2. Core the apples leaving the bottom solid. Heat honey, Calvados, and water in a small saucepan over low heat. Pour the sauce into each apple evenly. Distribute the 1/2 tbs. of butter into each apple evenly.

3. Place apples in a small baking dish. Bake in oven for 10 minutes at 350°F. Lower the temperature to 300°F and add the boudin blanc. Bake for another 10 minutes. Baste with the pan juices occasionally.

4. Serve the boudin with a baked apple and the truffle sauce.

Tips and suggestions:
Any mild sausage may replace the boudin blanc in this recipe.
Truffle bits are less expensive than whole truffles and work fine with this recipe. A less expensive alternative to the black truffles is black chanterelles.

Vegetable Farandole

Preparation: 5 minutes
Cooking: 10 minutes

1/2 cube chicken broth
1 zucchini
2 carrots
1 turnip
1 tbs. olive oil
1 tbs. goose fat
1 C. fresh peas
1/2 tbs. parsley
Pinch pepper

1. Bring water to boil with cube of chicken broth. Boil the zucchini whole for 3 minutes in boiling water and strain. Boil the carrots and turnip for 10 minutes in boiling water and strain. Let cool and slice into disks.

2. Add olive oil and goose fat to a hot sauté pan and add the boiled vegetables and peas. Sauté slightly with pepper and parsley for 2 minutes. Serve with the goose and gravy.

Pinot Noir Goose with Vegetable Farandole

"Gans im pinot noir met gemesle"
Oie au pinot noir et farandole de légumes

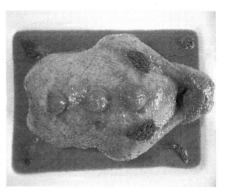

Geese have a special place in Alsace, not only for their liver, from which foie gras is made, but also for their succulent meat. Their only rival is the highly honored pig. Geese used to roam the villages in small flocks until the holidays approached, and housewives took them into their yards and some even into their kitchen to fatten them up. A roasted goose symbolizes winter celebrations in Alsace much like a turkey symbolizes Thanksgiving in the USA.

Preparation: 20 minutes
Cooking: 1 hour 45 minutes

Stuffing:
1 small yellow onion, chopped
1/2 C. morel mushrooms, fresh or bottled
2 tbs. mashed roasted chestnuts
1/4 C. walnut breadcrumbs
1/2 tbs purree de tomate
1/2 tsp. capers
1 tbs. parsley
1 tsp. chives
1/2 tsp. salt
1/2 tsp. pepper
1/4 tsp. Herbes de Provence
1/2 tbs. Poire Williams schnapps

Goose:
1 goose, cleaned and gutted
String to close the goose
1/2 tsp. salt
1/2 tsp. pepper
1 garlic clove
2 tbs. walnut oil
1/4 C. leeks, sliced
1 tomato, quartered
1 small yellow onion, sliced
1 pear, peeled and diced
1 shallot, sliced
1 bottle Pinot Noir
1 small branch of celery leaves
1/4 tsp. honey
1 cube of chicken broth
1/2 C. hot water
1/4 C. roasted chestnuts
1/4 C. morel mushrooms

1. Prepare the stuffing. Mix all the stuffing ingredients and use to stuff the goose. Sew the goose shut using the string.

2. Salt and pepper the outside of the goose. Cut the garlic in half and make a hole on each side of the goose with a knife and stuff the garlic inside. Place walnut oil in a caldron over high heat and brown the goose. Remove the goose and sauté the leeks, tomato, onion, pear, and shallot in the same pot until slightly caramelized.

3. Return the goose to the pot. Add a bottle of pinot noir, celery, and the honey. Cover and simmer for 1 hour. Dissolve the chicken cube in hot water. After 1 hour lower the heat to medium and add the chicken broth. Sauté for another 1/2 hour. You should have 1½ cups of sauce in the pot when finished cooking. You can check with a thermometer or knife to see if the meat is finished.

4. Remove the goose and strain the sauce. Add the morel and roasted chestnuts to the sauce and heat through. Keep warm and serve with the goose as gravy.

Tips and suggestions:
Another red wine may be used, as well as Riesling, to replace the Pinot Noir.

Cherry Schnapps with Fresh Munster Cream Cheese

"Sieskas met kirsch"
Fromage frais au kirsch

This cheese is taken early in the process of traditional Munster fabrication, before the cheese is salted and aged. It is similar to a cream cheese or ricotta in flavor and the consistency is soft.

Preparation: 5 minutes

3 C. fresh Munster cheese
1/4 C. granulated sugar
2 tbs. kirsch
1/2 C. crème fraîche (see recipe)

1. Place fresh Munster cream cheese in a serving bowl. Poke holes into the cheese with a toothpick or fork. Sprinkle sugar over the fresh cheese and drizzle the kirsch over the top. Cover with crème fraiche.

2. Serve cold with pear bread.

Tips and suggestions:
This may be mixed together to form a sweet cream if you prefer.
This is also traditionally served with cherries marinated in schnapps.

Spiced Pear Bread

"Baerewecke"
Pain aux poires confites

There is much more that just pears in this festive bread. It is traditionally served with schnapps for New Year's Eve to visitors passing by to wish them a happy New Year. It can keep for weeks, so you can make it well in advance.

Marinade: 1-2 days
Preparation: 2 hours
Baking: 1 hour

1 C. dried pears
3/4 C. dried apricots
3/4 C. prunes
1/2 C. dried figs
1/2 C. dates
1/3 C. dried apples
1/4 C. golden raisins
2 tbs. red raisins
1/3 C. almonds
3 tbs. hazelnuts
2 tbs. candied orange peel
2 tbs. candied lemon peel
3/4 C. pear schnapps
1/8 tsp. ground cloves
1/4 tsp. ground star anise
1/2 tsp. cinnamon
Pinch of nutmeg
1 tsp. lemon zest
1/4 C. sugar

Dough:
1/2 C. whole milk
2 tsp. dry yeast
1¼ C. flour
Pinch of salt
2 tbs. sugar
2 tbs. softened butter

1 egg yolk

Sugar syrup:
1/3 C. water
1/2 C. sugar

1. Chop the fruit and nuts roughly. You may need to soften some of the fruits in hot water in order to chop them. Cut the orange and lemon peel into pieces a little smaller than the rest. Mix with the pear schnapps, cloves, star anise, cinnamon, nutmeg, lemon zest, and sugar. Marinate for 1 to 2 days.

2. Strain the fruit and save the marinade for the dough.

3. Warm 1/2 cup of the milk and dissolve the yeast into it. (Be careful not to heat the milk too hot or it will kill the yeast.)

4. In a bowl, mix the flour, salt, and sugar with the yeast mixture. Work the softened butter into the dough. Stir until the dough separates from the bowl, adding more flour if necessary. Cover with a cloth and let rise in a warm place for 1 to 2 hours.

5. Mix in the fruit and nuts and form into a loaf. Place on a buttered baking sheet and brush egg yolk over the surface. Let rise for 2 hours in a warm place.

6. Bake for 50 to 60 minutes at 350°F until golden brown. Brush with sugar syrup after 30 minutes. Cover with wax paper if the pear loaf starts to burn.

Tips and suggestions:
Add a teaspoon of orange flower essence to the marinade if you can find it. Kirsch, Calvados, or brandy can replace the Poire William schnapps. You may use different combinations of fruits and nuts for this.

Onion Soup

"Zewelsupp"

Soupe à l'oignon

The best food is often the simplest!

Cooking: 40 minutes

3 large yellow onions
1 tbs. butter
2 C. beef broth
1/2 C. Gewürztraminer
1/8 tsp. parsley
2 eggs

1. Thinly slice the onions. Sautee the onions in butter over medium heat until caramelized.
2. Add beef broth, wine, and parsley. Simmer for 1/2 hour. Before serving, whisk eggs and add to soup while stirring until the eggs are cooked.

Tips and suggestions:

Any sweet white wine may be substituted for the Gewürztraminer.

Bitter Herrings

"Gereichertiheri"
Harengs saures

This is an after-hours snack used to help with the champagne hangovers.

Preparation: 2 minutes
Marinade: 8 hours

2/3 C. crème fraîche (see recipe)
1/4 C. dill pickles, chopped
1/4 tsp. pepper
1/2 tbs. honey vinegar
12 smoked herring filets

1.   Mix crème fraiche, pepper, pickles, and vinegar. Gently coat the herrings with this sauce.
2.   Marinate the herrings overnight.
3.   Serve with whole grain bread.

Tips and suggestions:
Be careful when handling the filets. They break apart easily.

Accordion

February

Venison Stewed in Wine

1,000 Flower Butter Leaf Salad with Honey Vinaigrette

Fennel and Zucchini Sautée

Spätzele

Apple, Sage, and Flower Donuts

Black Currant Sauce

Mardi Gras Donuts

Wine Suggestions
Meal—Aged Bordeaux or another Dry Red Wine
Dessert—Coffee with Schnapps

Cry of the Hunter

"Mer muss die feschter fiere wie se falle."
One must celebrate occasions as they arrive.

In Alsace, it is cold in February. There is a period between New Year and Epiphany where life slows down. I happened to ask Ben one evening what he used to do for fun during this time of year. He smiled at me like the Cheshire cat and said, "Ma chère amie, non, non, non! In Alsace we don't sit and count the baguettes all winter. When we are not on the streets protesting cigarette tax increases or decreases in vacation time from twenty-five to twenty-four days, we have a village dance! February is parfait! Everyone is looking for something to do before Carnival kicks in. It is not too difficult to gather together an impromptu orchestra and singers. One simply mentions that there will be schnapps flasks strategically stashed and casually mention some of the local specialties that the women are preparing. Yes, it is really quite simple, and with all the local villages doing the same, we keep ourselves quite busy." As it turned out, Ben sang in the choral society at these events along with his brother, Patrick. He recounted a story from one of these February evenings. According to Ben, he and Patrick were returning home after singing in the choral soceity of a neighboring village dance that started early in the day and lasted until the "petite" hours of the night. They had been quite impressed with their performance and were full of mirth as they drove their car through the forest of Petit-Pierre ("Little-Pete"), navigating a narrow stretch of dirt road known to be a good shortcut. It was dark that night, as many February's are, and there were no lights on the road except for their car. The local radio station was playing waltzes and Alsatian oldies, so Ben and his brother cranked up the radio and sang along, admiring their own talent, of course. They sang to the moon, they sang to each other, and they sang to memories of the girls who had watched them onstage with admiration throughout the night. Yes, it had been a successful evening. Suddenly, a stag, perhaps attracted by the beauty of their tenor voices, although more likely hoping to shut them up and bring peace back to the forest, gave an ultimate and supreme self-sacrifice and jumped out right in front of the car. Their singing passed from the low tones of the waltz on the radio to clear soprano duo to high-pitched screams as they slammed on the brakes to avoid disaster. The stag returned Ben's terror-ridden gaze with a fierce regard—or was it determination? Then there was an impact! SMASH! The stag rolled on the windshield and back onto the hood. The car came to a stop and everything fell silent. The courageous stag passed away with a sigh of satisfaction, having returned peace to the virginal forest. Patrick broke the silence by bursting into sobs, completely overwhelmed at the frailty of life. Ben, who it turns out is more pragmatic in nature, began calculating the number of meat tortes that he could make with the stag that probably weighed 300 kilos. As far as Ben was concerned, there was really only one option. They put the stag in the trunk and took it home.

Ben's eyes grew wide at the end of his retelling of the story, as he remembered the family dinners that February. "Ah! The recipes we made with that exquisite meat. We must put one in the book."

Carnival

Deer Stewed in Wine, 1,000 Butter Leaf Salad, Spatzele, Fennel and Zucchini Sautee

Venison Stewed in Wine

"Rehragout"
Civet de Cerf

Preparation: 10 minutes
Marinade: 8 hours
Cooking: 2 hours

1½ lbs. of venison leg meat
1 bottle of Pinot Noir
1 tsp. salt
1 tsp. pepper
1 carrot
1 celery branch
1 potato
1/4 C. fresh parsley
1/2 C. fresh thyme branches
2 bay leaves
1/4 C. butter
2 C. morel mushrooms
1 C. pearl onions
1/2 tsp. balsamic vinegar
1/2 C. cold butter cubed
1 tbs. cornstarch
1 tbs. crème fraîche (see recipe)

1. Mix the deer meat, wine, salt, pepper, carrot, celery, potato, parsley, thyme, and bay leaves. Marinate overnight.
2. Melt 1/4 cup of butter in sauté pan. Add morel mushrooms and onions. Sauté over medium heat until the onions caramelize. Remove the morels and onions and set aside.
3. Increase heat to high and add the marinated meat. Brown on all sides. Lower the heat to medium. Remove the potatoes from the marinade and discard. Add the marinade to the pan. Cover and simmer for 1 to 2 hours until the meat is cooked. Remove the meat and set aside.
4. Strain the sauce and return to the pan. Add balsamic vinegar. Reduce the liquid in half over high heat. Lower the heat and whisk in 1/2 cup of cold butter and then cornstarch. Whisk in crème fraîche before serving.
5. Serve the deer meat with morel mushrooms and sauce. Garnish with fresh thyme sprigs.

Tips and suggestions:
Beef may be substituted for the deer. If you are using a fatty piece, marinate it in the same way as the deer meat. If you use a lean cut, marinate it for just 1 hour or it may toughen.

1,000 Flower Butter Leaf Salad
with Honey Vinaigrette

"Gruenersalade met Honivinaigrette"

Salade verte aux mille fleurs à la vinaigrette au miel

Preparation: 5 minutes

1 head of butter leaf lettuce
Dijon vinaigrette (see recipe)
1 C. cherry tomatoes, cut in half
1/4 C. toasted pine nuts
Edible flowers for garnish (optional)

Tips and suggestions:
Replace the Dijon vinaigrette with another according to your taste.

1. Tear the lettuce into pieces and place in serving bowl and toss with vinaigrette.
2. Slice the cherry tomatoes in half and sprinkle over the top with the pine nuts. Garnish with edible flowers.

Fennel and Zucchini Sauté

"Fenschel met courgette"

Sauté de fenouil et de courgettes

Preparation: 5 minutes
Cooking: 5 minutes

1 fennel bulb
2 zucchinis
1 tbs. butter
1 tbs. olive oil
Pinch salt
Pinch pepper
1 tsp. thyme

Tips and suggestions:
Cabbage may replace the fennel.

1. Slice the fennel bulb into thin strips. Slice the zucchini into 1/2" discs.
2. Melt butter and olive oil in frying pan. Sauté the fennel over medium heat until it softens. Increase the heat and add the zucchini, salt, pepper, and thyme. Sauté until the zucchini colors. It should stay a little crispy.

Spätzele

"Spätzle"

Spatzele à l'alsacienne

The first pasta was probably made by mixing flour and water together and cooking the resulting mixture. The recipe for spatzele is similar to this and is probably the oldest pasta form in existence. The origin is not known.

Preparation: 15 minutes
Cooking: 10 minutes

5 eggs
2 egg yolks
1/4 C. water
Pinch nutmeg
Pinch salt
2½ C. flour
3 tbs. butter

1. Beat eggs, yolks, water, nutmeg, and salt. Add the flour while mixing until it forms a runny paste.
2. Boil water in a pan. Place a cheese grater over the pot and press the paste through the grater into boiling water, forming a type of noodle. Boil until the noodles rise to the surface. Rinse in cold water and drain.
3. Melt butter in saucepan and sauté the spatzele before serving.

Tips and suggestions:
To make the spatzele without a grater, use 4 eggs and roll the paste into long strips. Then cut into about 1" pieces, smooth the tips and boil in water.

Black Currant Sauce

Coulis au cassis

Cooking: 10 minutes

1 C. black currant berries
1/2 C. white wine
1/2 C. sugar
1/2 tsp. cornstarch
1/4 C. tawny port

1. Simmer black currant berries, white wine, and sugar in saucepan for 5 minutes. Pass through a strainer to remove any seeds and skins.
2. Dissolve cornstarch in the tawny port and add to the berry mixture. Heat the sauce again while stirring until the sauce thickens. Remove from heat and stir until room temperature.
3. Store in refrigerator until ready to use.

Tips and suggestions:
Raspberry, blueberry, apricot jams, or any fruit sauce may be used to replace the cassis.

Mardi Gras Donuts and Apple, Sage, and Flower Donuts

Mardi Gras Donuts

"Fassenachtskuechle"

Beignets de carnaval

D'bescht Koscht isch die, wo nit viel koscht!
The best food is the cheapest!

Preparation time: 1 hour
Cooking time: 10 minutes

1/4 C. butter
1/3 C. sugar
1 egg
1 tsp. lavender (optional)
1/2 tbs. orange flower water
1 tsp. brewers yeast
1/2 C. lukewarm milk
2 C. flour

Oil for frying
1 C. sugar
1 tsp. cinnamon

1. Mix the butter and sugar well. Stir in the egg, lavender, and orange water. Dissolve the yeast into the milk and stir into the butter mixture. Incorporate the flour. Cover and let stand in a warm area for 1 to 2 hours.

2. Roll on a floured board to a thickness of 1/2" and cut into triangles.

3. Fry in hot oil until golden. Place on a paper towel to remove extra oil.

4. Roll in cinnamon and sugar and serve warm.

Tips and suggestions:
Vanilla may be used to replace the lavender.

Apple, Sage, and Flower Donuts

"Apfelkuechle"

Beignets aux pommes, à la sauge et aux fleurs

Frying various fruits and flowers in a layer of dough was common practice in the Middle Ages.

Preparation: 10 minutes
Cooking: 10 minutes

4 apples
1/4 C. schnapps (optional)
Frying batter (see recipe)

1/2 C. powdered sugar
1 tsp. cinnamon
Black currant sauce (optional)

Sage and various edible flowers: elderberry, hibiscus, lavender, thyme, zucchini flowers, chamomile, etc.

1. Peel and core the apples. Cut into thick slices so that the core is in the center. Sprinkle the apples with schnapps and let soak for 10 minutes. Strain any extra liquid.
2. Heat oil until a bit of the batter bubbles and turns golden when dropped in.
3. Dip apple slices into the frying batter and then drop into the hot oil until golden brown. Remove from the oil and drain on a paper towel.
4. Sprinkle with sugar and cinnamon. Serve with black currant sauce.

Coat and fry the sage and flowers in the same manner.

Tips and suggestions:
Apricots and peaches are delicious substitutions for the apples.
Raspberry, blueberry, apricot jams, or any fruit sauce may be used to replace the black currant sauce.

Impressions

March

Flambéed Alsatian Pizza

Butter Leaf Salad with Garlic Vinaigrette

Baker's Stew

Apple Tart

Wine Suggestions
Appetizer—Reisling Wine
Meal—Reisling or Sylvaner Wine
Dessert—St. John's Walnut Liquor

Tarte flambée oven

Tarte Flambée Mystery (Flammekueche)

"Die Grosse wäre nit gross ohne die kläne."
The big would not be big without the small.

Karaoke has a certain allure in Alsace. One finds karaoke bars filled with smoke and regulars who normally don't dare sing even in the shower but suddenly find the courage to rise and sing their hearts out to traditional songs such as "O Mein lieber Bratwurst!" (Oh my dear bratwurst!) or "Schoener Kougelhopf!" (Lovely bread!), and, of course, an occasional European or American pop song. Ben is no exception. One evening, after I heard him rehearsing in his apartment next door, I asked if I could tag along. Ben responded with a big smile. "Mais oui! Of course you can come with me. I will introduce you to all my friends. You will like them very much. Come inside and sit down. Here's a glass of wine. You can help me with the Elvis Presley song. What does it mean—I'm all shook up? I am told that I pronounce the words very well."

Forty minutes and half a bottle of wine later, we were walking along the rue des Frères on our way to Bunny's, his favorite karaoke bar. Ben was still practicing his favorites when two young tourists walked up to us with lost looks on their faces. The skinny man with thick unruly brown hair and a tee shirt with a photo of a giant hamburger asked Ben timidly, "Excuse me, can you tell me where is a good place to try this local pizza you have here?" Ben, who is usually happy to help a confused tourist find his way, stiffened at the word "pizza," but maintained his composure and turned to me for a full translation. I told Ben that he wanted to know where they could find a good place to taste the pizza—uh—the tarte flambée. "Quoi (What)?!!" Ben asked. "What did they say? I don't understand." There was still a chance to escape the situation peacefully, until the thin man pointed in his tourist guide to the fateful words: "Tarte Flambée" (flammekueche). Ben grew pale and his breathing turned to a rasp. He was definitely irritated now. To an Alsatian, and even worse an Alsatian chef, calling a tarte flambée a "pizza" is the equivalent of asking for ketchup when served a rack of lamb roasted with prunes at Chez Panisse. A diplomatic incident. A fatal error. Ben fixated on the traveler with the gaze of a cobra and spoke with the force of a river breaking loose from its dam. "Jeune homme, tarte flambée IS NOT pizza! Primo, Italians have most likely stolen our recipe without being able to copy it correctly. Deuzio, here one never uses tomato sauce, quelle horreur! On the dough of the noble flammekueche, there is an exquisite mixture of fresh cream, bacon, and onions. Tertio, yes, pizzas and flammekueche are both made on a base of bread dough, but, but, BUT the flammekueche is never round like a pizza, it is rectangular. RECTANGULAIRE!" While speaking, Ben repeatedly traced a rectangle in the air with his fingers. The thin man, not understanding any words but rectangle, but nonetheless sufficiently frightened by the flood of words that fell on him from the originally nice-looking man, had already begun a slow retreat while his companion had disappeared without saying good-bye. They had no idea that this shaking red-faced Frenchman had a love for hotdogs with the yellow ketchup and soft buns that he tasted as a child in Florida. I realized that if Ben were suddenly on the streets in Florida, he would be the one approaching the locals searching for a hotdog. But I think he wouldn't make the mistake of calling it a taco.

Ben was in no shape to go sing karaoke, so I took him to a restaurant and appeased him by ordering some flammekueche. After a few bites he began to regain his composure as he took comfort in the fact that his grandfather was not there to witness the event, may he rest in peace. It was, after all, his grandfather who taught Ben how to make them when he was eight years old. As Ben began to reminisce, I started taking recipe notes. After all, flammekueche was a particular weakness of mine. Ben didn't seem to notice, as he was lost in the past. Learning how to make a flammekueche for petit Ben was no laughing matter. It was a rite of passage. Even though all the families in the village had a recipe for flammekueche, his grandfather told him with pride on the first day, "Only you will have my recipes after I die." And so the apprenticeship began—a sort of flammekueche boot camp. Grandpa was a strict and tough drill sergeant. They started at 6:00 in the morning with a bag of flour. His grandfather monitored, as Ben passed it through a sieve no less than five times. Then came the water exercise. The family recipe called for water from the river running along the edge of the farm and Ben was given a bucket with an implied command to double-time it. And most importantly, everything had to be mixed by hand. "Cest ça qui donne le goût!" (That's what gives it its flavor!) Ben's small hands worked the dough until his arms were covered in white sticky goo. Then came the final obstacle course. His grandfather picked up the dough and threw it on the table with a crushing force. The dough had to bounce three times on the table to pass the test. If not, he threw it in the dustbin and made Ben start over. It took three long, hot, sticky days before Ben succeeded. Each night his little arms ached, but he kept going because he wanted to make his grandpa proud. When he finally finished, they put the tarts in the family's large wood-burning oven. There was one for grandma, one for grandpa, and one with extra lardons for petit Ben.

Flambéed Alsatian Pizza

"Flammekueche"
Tarte flambée

Ben's grandfather used to say, "The devil is in the oven fire and you need to cook the flammekeuche quickly or he will eat it."

Preparation: 10 minutes
Cooking: 5 minutes

Pinch salt
Pinch pepper
1/2 tsp. flour
1/2 C. fromage blanc
(see fresh cream cheese recipe)
1/3 C. cream
1½ tsp. vegetable oil
1 large yellow onion
2/3 C. cubed smoked bacon.

1 Tarte flambée dough. (see recipe)

1. Preheat the oven to 575°F. Place the oven shelf in the lowest position.
2. Mix the salt, pepper, flour, fromage blanc, cream, and oil. Cut the onion in thin slices.
3. Roll the dough into a rectangle shape about 1/4" thick. Lay on a well-floured baking sheet. Press the edges slightly with your fingers. Spread the cream mixture over the rolled pastry, starting in the center and being careful to leave a half inch of the edge free. Sprinkle the sliced onion and bacon over the cream.
4. Place in the oven for 3 to 5 minutes until the crust is browned and the dough is cooked.

Tips and suggestions:
If you can't find fromage blanc, use crème fraîche for the whole amount or a mix with ricotta cheese.
Gratinée—Add 1/2 C. Emmental or Swiss cheese and increase the cooking by 1 minute.
Forestière—Add mushrooms of your choice. Be sure to sauté them if necessary.
Munster—Add Munster cheese and a pinch of cumin.

It is much better if you can bake this in a wood burning stone oven or even a very hot grill. It is important that the crust bake quickly or the toppings will burn.

Baker's Stew and Butter Leaf Salad with Garlic Vinaigrette

Butter Leaf Salad with Garlic Vinaigrette

"Gruenersalade met Knoblauchvinaigrette"
Salade verte à la vinaigrette à l'ail

Preparation: 5 minutes

Alsatian vinaigrette
1 small garlic clove, minced
1 head of butter leaf salad
1 tomato, diced

1. Mix garlic with Alsatian vinaigrette.
2. Toss with butter leaf lettuce and diced tomatoes and serve.

Baker's Stew

"Baeckeoffe"

Potée du Boulanger

This is traditionally a Monday dish. Sunday night the cook would prepare this recipe in the traditional terrine or dish and leave it at the baker's in the morning. She would then do laundry with the rest of the village women. The baker would place everyone's dish in the hot oven after he finished his regular baking, and the women picked up their cooked baeckeoffe later in the day.

Preparation: 20 minutes
Baking: 2½ hours

Slice of pork fat or bacon grease
6 firm potatoes
3 carrots
3 onions
1 tsp. salt
1 tsp. pepper
1/8 tsp. nutmeg
1 tbs. herbes of Provence
1 pinch sugar
1 tbs. chopped parsley
1/4 tsp. Worcestershire sauce
1 lb. beef
1 lb. pork shoulder or butt
1 lb. lamb shoulder
1 pig's foot (optional)
1 bottle of Sylvaner
2 shallots, sliced
2 cloves of garlic
3 bay leaves
1 tbs. thyme

2 C. flour
1 C. water
1 tsp. oil

Earthenware baking dish with lid

1. Grease the pot with the lard or bacon grease. Cut the potatoes, carrots, and onions into slices about 1/4 inch thick. Layer half of the potatoes in the bottom of the pot with 1/4 of the onions. Layer half the carrots next with another 1/4 of the onions. Sprinkle the salt, pepper, nutmeg, herbes de Provence, sugar, parsley, and Worcestershire sauce over the carrots.

2. Cut the meat into 1-inch cubes and place in the pot but don't let it touch the sides of the pot. Add wine to cover the meat. Add the shallots and garlic cloves. Lay the bay leaves and thyme over the top. Layer the rest of the onions, carrots, and potatoes.

3. Prepare a paste to seal the pot. Mix water into the flour until it forms a sticky paste.

4. Rub the oil along the edge of the lid and place the lid onto the pot. Mold the paste into a long strip and lay along the edge of the top of the pot, sealing it shut.

5. Heat the oven to 400°F. Place the pot into the oven and reduce the heat to 350°F. Cook for 2½ hours.

6. Remove from the oven and break the crust to open the pot. Make sure that the meat is cooked. If not, you can continue to bake in the oven without resealing the pot.

Tips and suggestions:
Traditionally, a pig's foot and tail are added to the pot to add flavor. I have only included a pig's foot, but you may substitute a couple slices of unsmoked bacon if you like. Any dry white wine may be substituted for the Sylvaner. A pressure cooker may be used instead of the earthenware baking dish, but the earthenware pot makes a nicer presentation at the table.

Apple Tarte

"Apfelkueche"
Tarte aux pommes

Tarts in Alsace distinguish themselves from the North American variety by not having a layer of dough on the top to cover the fruits. The tart is thus lighter and allows the fruit to express itself more.

Preparation: 15 minutes

Baking: 50 minutes

1 puff pastry (see recipe)
1/3 C. sugar
1/2 tsp. cinnamon
2 eggs
1/2 C. crème fraîche (see recipe)
1/2 tsp. vanilla
2 pinches nutmeg
4 pink lady apples

1. Preheat oven to 400°F and place the rack in the lowest position. Line a tart pan with wax paper. Lay the puff pastry over the wax paper and pinch the edges. Pierce the pastry with a knife evenly.
2. Mix a teaspoon of the sugar and a pinch of the cinnamon and set aside.
3. Beat the eggs slightly with the remaining sugar. Stir in the crème fraiche, vanilla, nutmeg, and the remaining cinnamon.
4. Peel, core, and slice the apples. Arrange the apple slices in the tart pan. Pour the cream mixture over the apples.
5. Bake in oven for 10 minutes until the crust begins to color.
6. Reduce the temperature to 350°F and sprinkle the sugar cinnamon mixture over the top. Continue to bake for another 40 minutes until the custard is done and the pastry is golden.
7. Serve warm or at room temperature.

Tips and suggestions:
You may use other apples as long as they are not too sour.
This doesn't need ice cream, but it doesn't hurt to have it. You may also mix some crème fraiche, sugar, and Calvados, and serve as a sauce.

Tarte flambée chez les Federlin

Street Singer

April

Cherry Soup

White Beans Simmered in Wine

Roasted Leg of Lamb

Goat Cheese with Roasted Garlic and Shallots

Frisée Salad

Easter Lamb Cake

Wine Suggestions
Meal—Morgon or Bordeaux
Dessert—Coffee with Cherry Schnapps

Haut-Koenigsbourg

The Sparclub

"Do läbt mer wie Gott im Fronkräch."
To live like God in France.

Frederic and I had just returned from visiting the nearby medieval castle of Haut-Koenigsbourg, when Ben passed by on his way to the Saturday market and asked if we wanted to go with him. "Avec plaisir! We love going to the market." I needed to buy some herbs from M. Metz, who ran a small organic herb farm in the Vosges Mountains, and who always asked about the varieties found in North America and offered explanations of the medicinal properties of the various herbs for sale. Frederic, on the other hand, was always happy to browse through the duck and cheese stalls, after which he usually had a look of satisfaction as he discretely carried a new bag of goodies. More often than not, we both passed by the escargot stall full of snail quiches, snail sandwiches, and garlic- and herb-buttered snails. We just weren't ready yet.

As we walked along the canal to the market, our conversation naturally centered on the impressive castle of Haut-Koenigsbourg. The castle is located at the top of a mountain in the Vosges that dominates the west side of the Rhine Valley. It is in amazing condition due to the restoration by the German Emperor William II of Hohenzollern, which was completed just before Alsace was passed back to the French after World War I. Like most Alsatians, Ben had visited the castle, but he said with a chuckle that he couldn't think about Haut-Koenigsbourg without thinking of his favorite cousin, Patrice. Patrice had two distinctive characteristics—his love and respect for food, and his biting wit.

Ben began to recount a story from his childhood concerning the Sparclub, the village organization that dedicated to encourage the leisure activities of the inhabitants. Practically everyone was a member. They would meet every Sunday after mass to pay their dues, which were promptly locked away in the safe behind the bar. Afterwards the adults would have a beer and play a friendly game of cards. Each year, the culmination of their efforts would end in a grand finale: a village day trip designed to broaden their collective awareness of Alsace and, of course, its gastronomy.

Over time, the Sparclub had become a sort of institution in the village, and its founders, Monsieur Matisse and Monsieur Kholur, were well respected. M. Matisse and M. Kholur were old childhood buddies who were seen together more often than with their wives, walking arm in arm through the streets of the village, talking and laughing wherever they went. It was impossible not to recognize them as they passed by, since their profile was somewhat distinctive. M. Kholur was blessed with a tall, thin, somewhat lurch-like physique, while M. Matisse was short and had taken on a sort of "robust" profile over the years. Ben knew them well, as he had spent many Sunday afternoons at the club, visiting with Patrice and watching the founders joke and play cards side by side.

Given the objective of Sparclub, it was inevitable that they would plan a day trip to the famous Haut-Koeningsbourg castle one April Saturday. Ben and Patrice boarded the chartered buses along with the rest of the village and made their way up the winding road to the castle. After having admired the drawbridge, fortified walls, winding paths, and guard towers, they sat down to dine at the large carved banquet table in the castle. The room was heated by an ancient traditional ceramic stove, with pigs and lambs roasting on a spit in the giant fireplace. The servers, dressed in medieval costume, filled their goblets with the local brew while the medieval ensemble played their lutes and flutes. Ben sat across from Patrice at the big table. They had been looking forward to the Sparclub excursion with anticipation, not only for running around the castle pretending to be Count Dracula, but also, if not more so, for the feast of medieval delicacies served in royal style. They were gastronomical soul mates. It didn't take long to pile their plates high with ham and roasted lamb while trying to communicate through their stuffed mouths. Their conversation was even more thwarted by the loud music and dancing going on around them, but they continued to grunt and laugh at each other's efforts. Patrice was eating, and when he was eating he was happy, and when he was happy, his entertaining sharp wit was in high form.

Soon, he had the telltale twinkle in his eye of a humorous anecdote, and Ben, not wanting to miss the jewel, strained to hear his words. Patrice was laughing with his mouth full and trying so hard to make the words clear that he couldn't swallow, and he didn't even think of spitting out the tasty roasted lamb, so he tried to speaking louder and louder. He was practically shouting when Ben finally heard, "Each Sparclub celebration, M. Kholur gets skinner and lankier." Just then, Ben noticed M. Kholur dancing with his wife right behind Patrice, and he tried to warn him to be discreet with a kick under the table that ended up tapping his mother's leg instead of Patrice's. Patrice, pleased with his wit, and oblivious to new attention from Ben's mother, made a big effort and howled across the table to Ben just as the dance ended, "And M. Matisse gets shorter and fatter! They're like Laurel and Hardy." The force of his voice echoed throughout the dining hall and everyone turned and looked at him in the stunned silence. Slowly, the butcher of the village started to chuckle in a low, rumbling tone. Ben's mother then let out a shrill snicker, after which everyone, including the band, burst out laughing. Everyone, that is, except M. Matisse, M. Kholur, and Patrice, who were instead turning bright red. M. Matisse, furious with indignation, pulled Patrice's ear until he let out a squeal from his still full mouth, and then loudly said, "And you look more and more like a silly roasted piggy!" The rest of the day was sprinkled with the stifled laughter of jolly villagers, save a few permanently red faces. The village shared a collective, although quiet, giggle over this for weeks as Patrice endured the sound of mysterious squeals in the school yard as well as M. Matisse and M. Kholur's ready announcement of their displeasure each morning as he passed by the bar on his way to school. Since then, Patrice continued to find himself in touchy situations due to his spontaneous wit, but he never, ever spoke with his mouth full again.

Cherry Soup

"Kirschesupp"
Soupe aux cerises

This is an old recipe that used to be served during the Christmas holidays.

Cooking: 30 minutes

2 C. red cherries
3 C. Pinot Noir
1 C. water
1 C. cherry juice (from jar of cherries)
2 pinches pepper
2 pinches salt
2 pinches sugar to taste
1 juniper berry - optional

6 slices walnut bread
2 tbs. butter

1. Heat cherries, wine, water, cherry juice, pepper, salt, sugar, and juniper berry in a saucepan. Cover and simmer for 1/2 hour.

2. Butter slices of walnut bread on both sides and sauté in saucepan until golden and crunchy.

3. To serve, place a slice of the walnut bread in each bowl and ladle the soup over the bread.

Tips and suggestions:
If making this in the summer, use fresh pitted cherries. You will need to add more sugar to taste. The cherry juice may be replaced with half water, half wine.
The juniper berry may be replaced with a pinch of thyme for a variation.

White Beans Simmered in Wine

"Wissi Bohne"
Haricots blancs

Marinade: 8 hours
Cooking: 30 minutes

3 C. dry white beans
1 tbs. olive oil
1 shallot, minced
1 garlic clove
1 small carrot, diced
1 tomato, diced
1 C. dry white wine
Pinch of salt
Pinch of pepper
Pinch sugar
Water

1. Cover the beans with warm water and soak overnight. Strain the beans and place in bowl.

2. Heat olive oil in pan. Add shallot and garlic and sauté until transparent. Remove from heat and add diced carrot, tomato, and beans.

3. Add wine and water to cover the beans. Add salt, pepper, and sugar. Stir gently and simmer for 20 minutes until the beans are easily pierced with a fork. Stir occasionally.

Tips and suggestions:
Use the carrots from the roasted lamb if possible.

Frisée Salad

"Gegruselter salad"
Salade frisée

Preparation: 5 minutes

1 head of frisée lettuce
Balsamic vinaigrette (see recipe)

1. Core lettuce and chop roughly. Toss with balsamic vinaigrette and serve.

Tips and suggestions:
Blue cheese and roasted shallots go well with this, as well as the goat cheese plate.

Roasted Leg of Lamb

"Gebrotener gigot"
Gigot rôti

Preparation: 10 minutes
Cooking: 1 hour

1/2 cube chicken bouillon
1 C. hot water
1 carrot
1 tsp. parsley
1 leg of lamb
1 C. butter, softened
9 large garlic cloves
1 tbs. herbes de Provence
1/2 tsp. salt
1/2 tsp. pepper
2 large onions
1 large tomato, halved

3 tbs. cold butter for the gravy

1. Preheat oven to 475°F. Place the bouillon cube, carrot, and parsley in hot water and simmer until carrots are soft. Remove carrots and set bouillon aside to use for basting the leg of lamb.

2. Remove extra fat from the leg of lamb. Set aside 2 tbs. of butter. Spread the rest over the entire surface of the lamb. Make 6 holes in the meat with a knife and place a garlic clove in each hole. Sprinkle with herbes de Provence, salt, and pepper.

3. Butter baking dish with 1 tbs. of butter and place the leg of lamb inside. Place onions, tomato, carrot, and 3 remaining garlic cloves around the lamb.

4. Bake in oven for 50 to 60 minutes. Add the bouillon into the pan and baste after the meat begins to brown (10 minutes). Baste the leg of lamb three or four times during cooking. After 20 minutes, slice the center about halfway down and insert 1 tbs. of butter. Reduce the temperature to 425°F and continue to cook until finished. Cover with foil if the roast starts to blacken.

5. Before serving, remove from the oven and press the sauce through a strainer. Simmer sauce in a pan over medium heat. Whisk in 3 tbs. of cold butter and remove from heat. Slice the lamb thinly at the table and serve the sauce as gravy with the lamb.

Tips and suggestions:
A beef or pork roast may be substituted for the lamb.

Goat Cheese with Roasted Garlic and Shallots

"Geisekäs-deller"

Plateau de fromages de chèvre

In Alsace, goat cheese is produced in the Vosges Mountains.

Preparation: 10 minutes
Baking: 20 minutes

1 head of garlic
1 tbs. olive oil
4 shallots, sliced
1 C. walnuts
2 tbs. honey
12 quail eggs (optional)
Fresh goat cheese, sliced
12 slices of bread

1. Separate garlic cloves, leaving the peel on. Toss in olive oil with the shallots and bake in oven at 225°F until nicely roasted.

2. Roast the walnuts on another baking sheet. Remove from oven and coat with honey. Keep warm.

3. Boil the quail eggs in water for 5 minutes.

4. Arrange goat cheese on a platter. Sprinkle the warm honey and walnuts over the fresh goat cheese. Serve with roasted garlic, shallots, and bread.

Tips and suggestions:
An assortment of goat cheese may be included for variety.
You may roast the garlic and shallots in a covered saucepan over low heat as well. Sweet onions may be used to replace the shallots.

Easter Lamb Cake

"Osterlamele"

Agneau Pascal

This cake is traditionally baked in a lamb-shaped mold, symbolizing the Sacrificial Lamb. For about a week in April the bakery windows are full of these lamb-shaped cakes. Ceramic artisans in Alsace continue to make molds in the shape of lambs as well as many other traditional baking potteries.

Preparation: 20 minutes
Baking: 45 minutes

1 C. cherries
1/2 C. kirsch

2 eggs
8 egg yolks
1 C. sugar
1 tsp. vanilla
1 tsp. lemon zest
8 egg whites
1/2 tsp. vinegar
1½ C. flour
2 tbs. cornstarch
1/4 C. warm melted butter

1/3 C. powdered sugar

Whipped cream or crème fraiche

1. Preheat oven to 350°F. Butter and flour a cake mold. Use one in the shape of a lamb if available.

2. Mix the whole eggs, egg yolks, and sugar with a whisk until the sugar dissolves. Heat in a double boiler, whisking constantly until the eggs form a ribbon. (A thick steam of liquid drops from the whisk when you lift it out of the sauce. The eggs should be hot but not curdled.)

3. Remove from heat, add the vanilla and lemon zest. Whisk until the mixture cools.

4. Whisk egg whites with vinegar until they form stiff peaks. Fold into the egg yolks mixture.

5. Mix the flour and cornstarch and fold into the egg batter along with the warm butter. Stir just until the ingredients are mixed.

6. Bake in the oven for 45 minutes until golden.

7. Sprinkle with powdered sugar. Serve with cherries and whipped cream.

Tips and suggestions:
If you have lumps in your sauce after step 2, run the sauce through a strainer.
To see if the cake is done baking, poke it with a toothpick. If it comes out clean it is done.
Brandy may be used to replace the kirsch.
This may be served with a vanilla cream, chocolate sauce, or a simple lemon icing instead of the cherries and truffles.

Gargoyle Soldier

May

Riwele Dumpling Soup

Dandelion Salad

Alsatian Farmer's Pie

Bennara Damson Plum Cake

Wine Suggestions
Meal—Pinot Noir or Beaujolais-village
Dessert—Coffee with Schnapps

Ben's Military Service

"Besser met de Gläser onstosse als met de kepp."
It's better to clink glasses than heads.

Since the dawn of time, Alsace has been the epicenter of many European wars. The Celts, Romans, and Germans all fought for its control. The sons of the great king Charlemagne divided his empire into three parts with Alsace ("Lotharingia") in the center. In the mid-eighteenth century, Louis XIV, the king of France, seized Strasbourg and made it a part of kingdom of France. And until very recently it has been the prized territory in wars between Germany and France in 1870–1871, 1914–1918, 1939–1945.

After World War II, Allied Forces were stationed in Alsace and this of course meant Americans were around. Older men here still bear witnesses to this period in history and talk for hours about the joy of the war being over, the sadness of human tragedies that many families suffered (Alsatian youth were forcefully drafted into the German Wehrmacht and many died on the Russian front), and gratitude for the bravery of the many soldiers with that funny white elastic bread.

Ben's mother learned to make desserts with that square bread that was handed out to the village by the soldiers. For Ben's mother, this new bread was delicious and sweet, just as the baguettes were to so many of the soldiers. She became so fond of using the bread that some of recipes were written into the treasured family cookbook. Many of the American bases remained open for years, and Ben recalls spending many a summer afternoon watching US soldiers practice parachute maneuvers in an open field near his village. One soldier stayed even longer—he married a woman from the next village and opened a bar, where he hosted annual reunions for his platoon. Like the Germans and the French, Americans became a part of the landscape of Alsace. Today, there are no American bases there; only the French remain separating the French/German border.

Military service was still mandatory in France until just a few years ago. When Ben was growing up, every man in France was required to serve one year after graduating high school. At eighteen, he followed the rest of the men his age to a military base near Colmar, thus separating for the first time from his mother, his village, his buddies, and most importantly, delicious home cooking. Upon their arrival, Ben's new sergeant, endowed with a large belly and a red face, informed his new troop, "You are all now like my own little children, weak and small, but I'm going to make men out of you!" Needless to say, the sergeant's nurturing came as a shock. Not only did he not give Ben the good night kiss his mom gave him, but he made Ben and his troop crawl in the mud—before sunrise! After their morning mud crawl, they then ran 10 km to the nearby mountain and took a brisk stroll to the top. Ben, who was not, to put it mildly, athletically inclined, suffered. And not being able to convince anyone that his fake cough was real and that he needed to spend time at the nurse's station resting, his only hope left was the prison. He calculated that all it would take to get there was to sufficiently irritate the sergeant. Ben had a natural aptitude for this and finally the day arrived. The sergeant, glowing red with anger, had had enough of Ben's shenanigans and sent him off to military prison for fifteen days.

Ben told me that the prison wasn't all that bad. In fact, the bed was comfortable and had clean pressed sheets. The cell was rather roomy, and there were magazines to read. When he was first escorted to his cell, Ben was very satisfied with the results of his efforts and thought to himself, "Fifteen days of lazy vacation, what a paradise! No jogging, no crawling in mud!" He hadn't yet discovered the terrible secret of French military prisons and their vast knowledge of French psychology. They had no need to break their unruly men through physical discomfort and boredom when they could use gastronomical misery! Here, one did not need harsh, physical exercise and verbal abuse to straighten out new recruits, but rather the subtle and much more effective torture of the spoilt and weak taste buds. Yes, this was a tried and tested method of discipline. A French soldier will do pushups in mud without much problem as long as he knows there will be a sandwich of duck pâté and a glass of wine at midday. The "Indestructible Sandwich" developed by the American army scientists, designed to stay fresh for literally three years under extreme climatic conditions, would fly like a lead balloon in the French army. The clever military prison brass understood the Frenchmen state of mind. As much as Ben's cell was comfortable, the food was repugnant. For starters, the bread was not the nice baguette that one usually finds in France, but a piece of rancid, moldy bread. Everything else— beef, potatoes, and cabbage—was simply boiled in water with no herbs or seasonings. There was no hint of wine or chocolate. No ham. No fresh cream. Rumor had it that the cook was an Englishman especially brought over to work in the prison kitchens. And the cruelest torture of all was that this food was found in abundance—there was more than enough to keep the soldiers coherent and aware of their misfortune. After fifteen days of boiled beef, Ben had lost twenty pounds. He had large bags under the eyes and a painful stare. He was a changed man. He now understood the importance of a meat tort in his life. He would never take it for granted again. He was going to obey the sergeant completely, he would crawl in mud with a smile, run 11 km each morning, he would do whatever it took to advance in rank. He would become sergeant himself and obtain the most valued prize the army had to offer: A seat at the officers' dining table.

Cannons of Haut-Koenigsbourg

Riwele Dumpling Soup

"Riewelesupp"
Potage aux riwelles

This is a simple beef broth with small dumplings. Riwele is basically the same type of pasta as spatzele, except that the pieces are smaller and not fried.

Preparation: 10 minutes
Cooking: 10 minutes

1 C. flour
2 eggs
Pinch of salt
2 liters of beef stock
Pinch of nutmeg
Pinch of pepper
1 carrot
1/2 tsp. chopped parsley

1. Mix the flour, eggs, and salt. Knead the dough and roll into a long thin strip about 1/4" thick. Cut into small pieces and roll between your hands to shape into small oblong dumplings.

2. Bring the beef stock to a simmer with the nutmeg, pepper, and carrots. Add the dumplings. Simmer for 10 minutes until the dumplings rise to the top.

3. Remove the carrot and add parsley. Serve warm.

Tips and suggestions:

Be sure to use a good beef stock for this recipe. If you are using bouillon cubes, use 1 chicken cube, 1 beef cube and 1/2 veal cube.

Chervil may be added along with the parsley according to taste.

Dandelion Salad

"Pissenlit salad"
Salade de pissenlits

Yes, you can eat dandelions, but it is the green or white leaves leaves that we use in Alsace, where you can buy them at the store like lettuce. However, Ben remembers gathering them in the countryside for his mother and sometimes selling them at the market for extra cash.

Preparation: 5 minutes
Cooking: 5 minutes

One head of dandelion leaves (white or green)
1/2 onion, thinly sliced
1/4 C. bacon (optional)
1 egg, hard-boiled
Dijon vinaigrette (see recipe)

Blue cheese
Walnuts

1. Wash and tear the dandelion leaves into pieces. Sauté bacon and slice the egg.
2. Mix vinaigrette and toss with onion and dandelion leaves. Garnish with bacon and egg.
3. Serve alongside a plate of blue cheese and walnuts.

Tips and suggestions:
I recommend trying this salad if you can find dandelion leaves. It is not a good idea to pick them from your yard, especially if you or your neighbors use pesticides such as weed killer. If you can't find them, you can use a mixed lettuce salad instead.

Alsatian Farmer's Pie, Dandelion Salad and Riwele Dumpling Soup

Alsatian Farmer's Pie

"Fleiseltourte"
Tourte à la viande

The tradition of meat pies in Alsace can be dated back to the eleventh century by remarks of pope Leo IX, who was quite fond of this dish from his hometown in Alsace. Every family has a recipe that is handed down through the generations. This is Ben's handed down to him from his grandmother to his mother to him. We have no idea how far back it dates.

Preparation: 30 minutes
Marinade: 1 day
Cooking: 40 minutes

2 large garlic cloves, cut in half
1 whole clove
1 bottle dry red wine
3/4 lb. pork, diced
3/4 lb. beef, diced
1 tsp. salt
1/4 tsp. pepper
1 tsp. Worcestershire sauce
1/8 tsp. nutmeg
1 onion, diced
1 carrot, chopped
1 tbs. parsley
1 shallot, minced

1 short crust pastry (see recipe)
1 puff pastry (see recipe)
1 egg
Pinch of sugar

1. Prepare the marinade. Pierce one of the garlic pieces with the clove. Mix the wine, meat, salt, pepper, Worcestershire sauce, nutmeg, onion, carrot, garlic, parsley, and shallot. Cover and let marinate overnight in the refrigerator.

2. Preheat the oven to 400°F.

3. Roll the short crust pastry and the puff pastry separately on a floured surface. They should each be the size of a tart pan. Place the short crust pastry on a floured baking sheet.

4. Drain the meat mixture and set aside 2 tbs. of the marinade. Spread the meat around the center of the short crust pastry, leaving at least an inch at the edge of the pastry. Mix the egg and sugar. Brush the edge of the pastry with the egg mixture.

5. Cover with the puff pastry and seal the border of the two pastries well. Cut a 1/2-inch hole in the center of the top of the pie. Roll the discarded pastry into a strip and attach around the hole in the top of the pie, making a chimney. Brush the egg mixture over the top of the pastry, including the seam, and lightly cut a pattern in the top of the pastry, making sure to pierce the crust a little for steam vents.

6. Place in the oven for 10 minutes until the pastry starts to color. Lower the oven temperature to 325°F and add the 2 tbs. of the marinade through the chimney. Continue to bake for a half hour until the bottom of the torte is golden.

Tips and suggestions:
The meat may be ground or chopped. The pastry may be entirely "short crust" if you prefer.
The city of Munster has its own special meat pie. It is similar to the recipe above, but the meat is generally ground pork, and the wine for the marinade is white. They also add a crumbled dry roll to the meat mixture.

Bennara Damson Plum Cake

Bennara Damson Plum Cake

"Bennara Zwetschgenstolle"

Gâteau Bennara aux quetsches

This cake batter is a creation of Ben's, and therefore modern Alsatian cuisine. He has been begged and bribed to divulge the secret, but has resisted until now. We hope you enjoy it. For this meal, we've added damson plums. Damsons are a small purple plum that taste similar to sour cherries. They are widely used for tarts, puddings, and, of course, schnapps fabrication.

Marinade: 8 hours
Preparation: 10 minutes
Baking: 50 minutes

1 jar of damson plums preserved in syrup
1/2 C. of damson plum schnapps
1/2 C. plain yogurt
1 C. sugar
1 tsp. vanilla
1/4 C. milk
1/4 C. vegetable oil
Juice of 1/2 lemon
1 tsp. melted butter
1½ C. flour sifted
1 tbs. + 1 tsp. baking powder
3 eggs

Butter and flour to prepare the pan
Vanilla ice cream (optional)

1. Drain the damson plums and set aside the syrup. Stir in the schnapps and let marinate overnight in the refrigerator. Drain the schnapps and let dry on a towel. Add the leftover schnapps to the saved syrup.
2. Preheat oven to 300°F. Butter and flour a 9"x9" baking pan.
3. In a bowl, whisk yogurt, sugar, and vanilla well. Stir in milk and oil. Stir in lemon juice and butter. Mix baking powder and flour and stir into the batter. Stir in 1 egg at a time. Mix well.
4. Place plums in the bottom of the prepared baking pan. Pour batter over the plums and bake in the oven for 50 minutes until golden brown. Poke the center of the cake with a toothpick. If it comes out clean, it is done. Cool and turn upside down onto a serving platter to remove from pan.
5. In a small saucepan, reduce schnapps syrup by half. Serve cake with reduced syrup and a scoop of vanilla ice cream (optional).

Tips and suggestions:
You may use many fruits for this recipe, such as prunes, apricots, cherries, and mirabelles. The liquor may also be changed accordingly.

Monastery Courtyard

June

Ill River Pike with Riesling Cream Wine

Tomato and Gruyére Salad

Fresh Egg Pasta

Vanilla Cream

Beggerman's Cake

Wine Suggestions
Meal—Riesling or Pinot Gris Wine
Dessert— Schnapps

The Sisters of the Mendiant

"Verboteni Frucht schmeckt am beschte"
Forbidden fruits are the most appetizing.

One day, while walking down the rue du 22 novembre for a morning café au lait, an unusual and enticing thing in a bakery window caught my eye. I had a habit of gazing at the multitude of pastries in pastry shop windows just begging me to bring them home. This time it was a small oval cake stuffed with apples and cherries and exuding a delicious air of cinnamon that was whispering to me with a compelling voice. Who could have resisted? I was just a mere human!

Later that day as I unpacked my new treasure, Ben knocked on the door and came in to visit. He immediately surmised the situation and exclaimed, "You have a mendiant! Ohh la la. They are delicious, but dangerous. They remind me of when I was in the convent." He lost his train of thought, as would anyone looking at a mendiant, but it was too late, I was already on the case. "In the CONVENT?" I asked. "Ben, you've been keeping secrets. I don't understand. The French nuns can't be that progressive!" Ben snapped back to reality and chuckled for a good few minutes until we were both bent over with laughter at the image of Ben in a habit hanging out with the sisters. "No, no, no, I worked in the kitchen," he managed to say. "Oh goodness. Let me explain. But hey, mendiant tastes better when you share it."

As we ate several thick slices, Ben told me about his work in a convent outside of Strasbourg that shelters a small community of nuns. Despite the small size and benevolent nature of the community, working for the sisters was no cakewalk. The meals were regarded as a time of devotion. True, the sisters took vows of poverty, chastity, and obedience, but by no means did they refuse God's gift of nourishing food! This convent was not the kind of austere order giving up all the joys of this world, but rather considered it a duty to honor the Lord according to their humble capacities. And included in their humble capacities were refined and subtle palates. Their palates were capable of tracking down the slightest piece of truffle hidden in a cauldron of soup, as a hunting dog is capable of tracking a partridge in a thick shrub. The sisters knew what was good. One did not give them canned raviolis or powdered soups from a bag without risking indignant glares in place of their usual welcoming smile.

When Ben started working there, the convent already had several cooks overly dependent on frozen and instant meals, and the sisters were getting restless. This manner of buying industrial, prepackaged, and precooked products to reduce the costs had always grated at Ben, but he needed the job, so he kept quiet and defrosted the tomatoes. Added to this aggravation were Fridays, when meat was taken off the menu. Those days, the meal was a veritable cross to bear that generally consisted of a bowl of clear vegetable soup accompanied by a small whole wheat roll. However, suffering does have its limits, and the limit at the convent on Fridays was dessert. After all, there was some justification. Desserts were certainly meatless, and they had the perfect one to ease their conscience: a dessert made up of an

78

enormous slice of the appropriately named mendiant (beggar). The mendiant is a cake of leftovers, therefore, a cake of the poor, and, therefore, fitting for meatless Fridays. It wasn't their fault that the cake tended to be rich with fruit and eggs, soaked with schnapps, and drowned in crème anglaise.

One such Friday—one could always tell when it was Friday by the way the sisters would walk through the corridors with hungry eyes—the precooked mendiants were delivered to the kitchen, and Ben saw that, catastrophically, they were dried out and hardened. "Aie, aie, aie, this will not do," Ben thought to himself, as he realized that the sisters could crack. The mendiant was their only beacon of hope at the end of a long Friday. He imagined the sisters capable of rioting in the kitchen, demolishing everything in their fury, like a band of prisoners in riot, throwing over the refrigerator to find the pâté and crème puffs, seizing cooks as they fled, and inflicting on them a penitence of rosaries, chaplets, and prayers to say.

Urgently, with sweat on his forehead and a lump in his throat, Ben sought a solution to avoid the impending catastrophe. Finally, he realized that the only way to keep his job and perhaps his right to communion was to remake the mendiants himself. In a flurry, Ben started preparing the mendiants, ripping up any old loaves and half-eaten kougelhopfs he could find and throwing them together with milk, eggs, and fruit. It was an awesome sight. He was spurred on by fear and inspired at the chance to really bake. He was soon adding a pinch of this and a little of that, although as quickly as possible, until a lovely cinnamon and cherry aroma began to emerge from the kitchen's old oven. Yes, he would live to tell the tale.

The following Monday, the mother superior called Ben into her office. He had noticed that she ate multiple slices of mendiant on that fateful Friday, and Ben was sure that she enjoyed it. She gave him a grandmotherly smile as he entered the room and said, "Blessed young man, you have a calling! From this day forward, no more dessert will be ordered from that wayward bakery. Ben, I'm putting you in charge of the kitchen. Everything is to be done in-house! God bless you, my son!"

Mont St-Odile

Tomato and Gruyère Salad

"Tomatesalad"

Salade de tomates

Marinade: overnight

Preparation: 5 minutes

Alsatian vinaigrette (see recipe)
1 bay leaf
6 tomatoes, sliced
1 C. Gruyère cheese, sliced
3 sweet pickles, diced
Pinch thyme
Pinch parsley
1 tbs. fresh basil

Tips and suggestions:
Dill pickles may be used to replace the sweet pickles.

1. Marinate bay leaf in vinaigrette overnight.
2. Arrange sliced tomatoes on a platter. Sprinkle cheese, pickles, thyme, parsley, and basil over the top.
3. Remove bay leaf and drizzle vinaigrette over the salad. Serve.

Ill River Pike with Cream Sauce

"Hechtfilet üss de Ill"

Filet de brochet de l'Ill à la crème

The Ill is the river that flows through Strasbourg. It is well-known for its pike fish. As a result the region has developed a variety of delicious recipes for this fish. It is said that in 1744, a thirty-six-pound pike fish was caught during a festival honoring King Louis XV. Of course, wherever there are fish and fishermen, there are legends.

Preparation: 10 minutes Baking: 20 minutes	1. Preheat oven to 400°F. Butter baking dish with half of the butter.
	2. Gut and scale the pike fish.
1 whole 3-lb. pike fish 1½ C. Paris mushrooms 1½ C. chanterelle mushrooms 2 shallots, diced 2 tbs. butter 1 tbs. olive oil 2 C. Riesling 1/2 tsp. salt 1/8 tsp. pepper 1/4 tsp. nutmeg Half of a cube of chicken bouillon 1/2 C. fresh parsley 2 C. broccoli 1 tbs. lemon juice 1/4 C. cream 2 tbs. crème fraîche (see recipe) Almond slices to cover the eyes	3. Sauté the mushrooms and shallots in the remaining butter and olive oil until they begin to color slightly. Remove the mushrooms and shallots from the pan and set aside for later. Deglaze the pan with Riesling, setting aside 1 tbs. for later. Add salt, pepper, nutmeg, chicken bouillon, and parsley. Simmer for 5 minutes. 4. Lay the pike in baking dish and cover with the wine sauce. Bake in oven for 20 minutes until done, basting occasionally. After the first 10 minutes of baking, add mushrooms, shallots, and broccoli to the pan and sprinkle the lemon juice over the pike. 5. Remove the pike from the oven and pour the sauce into a saucepan. Reduce by half. Remove from the heat and whisk in cream and crème fraîche. Sprinkle 1 tbs. of Riesling over the hot pike and cover the eyes with almonds. Serve with sauce, mushrooms and broccoli.

Tips and suggestions:
Pike filets may be substituted for the whole fish. Other fresh water fish may be used as well, such as trout or sander.
This is traditionally served with egg noodles, using the cream sauce to flavor the noodles as well as the pike.
Any white wine may be substituted for the Riesling.

Fresh Egg Pasta

"Selbschtgemachti Nüdle"
Nouilles alsaciennes

This dish most likely found its way from Italy to Alsace after the Thirty Years' War. A monk in Lucelle Abbey near Mulhouse in southern Alsace recorded it in 1671.

Preparation: 10 minutes
Cooking: 4 minutes

6 eggs
1/2 tsp. salt
1 tbs. honey vinegar
2 tbs. water
3 C. wheat flour
1½ C. semolina flour
1 cube chicken broth
1 tbs. butter

1. Mix together eggs, salt, vinegar, and water.
2. Mix wheat flour and semolina flour in a large bowl. Make a well in the center and add the egg mixture. Stir until the dough forms a ball, adding more water if necessary. Knead the dough for 5 minutes.
3. Roll into 4 balls. On a floured surface, roll out each ball of dough and cut into strips about 1/2 inch wide. Let dry on a floured cloth for a half hour.
4. Boil water with cube of chicken bouillon. Add pasta and boil for about 4 minutes until done. Drain.
5. To serve, sauté in butter and use a fork to roll servings into a nest shape.

Tips and suggestions:
This pasta may be dried and used later. If using the dry pasta, you will need to allow about 20 minutes boiling time. Be careful not to overcook the pasta.
If you are short on time you may substitute store bought egg noodles.
If you have the time, let the pasta rest for 1 hour, covered with a slightly damp cloth, before rolling in order to allow the consistency to develop.

Vanilla Cream

"Vanille crème"
Crème à la vanille

Preparation: 5 minutes
Cooking: 15 minutes

4 egg yolks
1/3 C. sugar
1½ C. whole milk
1/2 tsp. vanilla
1 tbs. kirsch

1. Mix egg yolks and sugar until mixture turns light yellow and creamy.
2. Heat milk in a double boiler. Pour hot milk into the egg yolk mixture while whisking constantly.
3. Return mixture to double boiler and heat while whisking until cream thickens. It is ready when it coats the back of a spoon.
4. Remove from heat and add vanilla and kirsch. Stir to cool. When at room temperature, cover and place in refrigerator to cool further.

Tips and suggestions:
A brandy of your choice or orange juice may be used to replace the kirsch.
The key to this recipe is heating the egg yolks slowly and cooling slowly so that the egg yolks don't harden or separate.

Beggarman's Cake

Beggarman's Cake

"Bettelmann"
Mendiant

Es isch nit alle Daa Sunndaa!!
It's not Sunday every day!'

Preparation: 1 hour
Marinade: 8 hours
Baking: 1 hour

1/2 lb. apples, plums, and apricots
1/2 lb. cherries
1/2 C. kirsch
3 tbs. butter
2 C. whole milk
1/3 C. sugar
1 old baguette (dry), cut in pieces
4 egg yolks
1 tsp. vanilla
1½ tsp. cinnamon
Pinch of nutmeg
Pinch of salt
4 egg whites
1/4 tsp. lemon juice
1/2 C. breadcrumbs

1. Chop apples, plums, and apricots into large bite-sized pieces. Mix with cherries and schnapps. Marinate overnight in refrigerator.

2. The next day, drain fruit and save liquid. Melt 1 tbs. of butter in a small saucepan and sauté fruit slightly until any extra liquid is evaporated. Be careful not to break fruit apart. Remove fruit and let dry.

3. Place bread in a large bowl. Heat milk and half of the sugar without boiling. When the sugar is dissolved, remove from heat and cool. Add egg yolks, vanilla, 1 tsp. cinnamon, nutmeg, salt, and the leftover fruit marinade. Pour the milk mixture over the bread. Mix together with your hands, breaking the bread into small pieces to form a rough batter. Let the batter stand for 1 hour.

4. Butter ceramic baking dish with 1 tbs. of butter and preheat oven to 300°F.

5. Whip egg whites with lemon juice until foamy. Add the rest of the sugar and continue whipping until firm. Fold the egg whites into the batter. Pour batter into buttered baking dish and place fruit throughout the batter, using a knife to sink the fruit. Save some fruit for garnish.

6. Mix breadcrumbs with the rest of the cinnamon and sprinkle over the top. Dot with the remaining tablespoon of butter and place in oven for 50 to 60 minutes. Pierce the middle with a knife or toothpick; if it comes out clean the cake is done.

7. Serve cold or warm with fruit garnish and vanilla crème.

Tips and suggestions:
You may substitute a Calvados or brandy for the kirsch. The fruit may vary according to taste.

Canal Reflections

July

Potato Salad

Celery Root Salad

Charcuterie Platter

Carrot Salad

Cherry Tomato Cherry Salad

Cervelas Sausage Salad

Emmental Cheese Salad

Fois Gras Tourt

Strawberries with Alsatian Cream

Hazelnut Tart

Wine and Beer Suggestions
Appetizers—Cherry Schnapps Lemonade
Meal—Gewürztraminer Wine or Kronebourg Lager

Bicycle and Dog

Salad in Alsace, a Misunderstood Vegetable

"Alles het an Anfang une e End, nur e Knackwurscht het zwei End."
Everything has a beginning and an end, only a sausage has two ends!
"E Biffdeck so gross wie e Abtrittdeckel macht dem kenn Ongscht."
A steak the size of a toilet lid doesn't scare him.

In Alsace, the green leaf does not generally take center stage. It rarely plays the starring roll on the table, as is the case of those ill-fated regions afflicted by the plague of Nouvelle Cuisine where one is served three leaves of lettuce, two baby carrots, one tomato slice, and a radish with a rutabaga purée in disguise as— Lord help us!—the "plat de résistance." No, in Alsace, a salad is generally a solid meal of its own.

I learned this one hot summer day when Frederic went off to work, and Ben and I went out to lunch. All of us were looking for some air-conditioning and shade from the blazing sun. We were feeling sluggish from the torrid heat and wanted to eat light, so Ben, who is by no means an amateur of the green leaf, ordered a salad: "La salade royale." I naively followed suit and soon realized the meaning of ordering a salad in a restaurant that honored tradition. The first clue of the impending drama I was in for was the burly arms of the waiter. I thought he must have been doing this as a side job while waiting to make it big in action movies until I noticed him bent under the effort of carrying our plates of salad to the table. Ben seemed only mildly taken aback as the waiter placed the plates in from of us. I, however, was astonished at the size of our plates. They were of astonishing volume and one could see piled from top to bottom three slices of pâté, torte as thick as a thumb and as long as a hand, five pieces of roasted pork thinly sliced—that is to say about a good centimeter thick, some fried knacks—hotdog-style sausages, enough bacon to reconstitute an entire pig, fresh sour cream, shredded celery root, boiled potatoes, and finally, to decorate the plate, a single leaf of lettuce. The whole salad probably could have nourished a polar explorer during three long days walking alongside his huskies toward the South Pole.

I was speechless and a little terrorized. I looked over at Ben, only to realize that he was deeply touched and was holding back tears of pride at the sight of a compatriot thus defending the noble tradition. We fought long and hard to finish the salad. It was each man for himself but it wasn't long before the bacon and celery root knocked me to the floor. Ben, on the other hand, was a born prizefighter and he only dropped his fork once before knocking out the last of the knacks in the third round. He then loosened his belt three notches and leaned back, tired but blissful, like a groggy boxer. The owner, who anxiously watched the course of the match, came to see us at the end of the meal. He honored Ben by speaking Alsatian and politely asked, "Was that enough, Monsieur? Perhaps dessert?"

Charcuterie Platter

"Wurstteller"
Assiette de charcuterie

Preparation: 5 minutes

Goose rillettes
Cured pork (jambon, proccuito)
Dry salted sausage (salami)
Pickles
Capers
1 baguette, sliced

1. Arrange on serving tray. Serve cool.

Tips and suggestions:
This may be a variety of cold meats according to your tastes and availability. "Goose rillettes" is shredded goose meat mixed with goose fat and spices.

Carrot Salad

"Galorewe salad"
Salade de carottes

Preparation: 10 minutes

6 large carrots
1/2 C. Alsatian vinaigrette (see recipe)
1 tsp. crème fraîche (see recipe)
1 tbs. parsley

1. Finely grate the carrots.
2. Stir in the vinaigrette, crème fraiche, and parsley.

Tips and suggestions:
This may be made the day before.

Celery Root Salad

"Celeri salad"

Salade de céleri

Preparation: 10 min.

1 head of celery root
Juice of 1/2 lemon
1 C. Alsatian vinaigrette (pg. X)
1 tbs. parsley
1/2 C. crème fraîche (pg. X)

1. Cut the celery root in quarters. Peel the skin until no dirt is showing. Wash and grate finely.
2. Squeeze the juice of 1/2 lemon over the celery and stir well. Add the vinaigrette and parsley. Let set overnight in refrigerator.
3. Stir in crème fraîche and serve.

Tips and suggestions:
The celery salad may be prepared the night before and the crème fraiche added before serving.

Emmental Cheese Salad

"Schwitzerkäs salad"

Salade à l'emmental

Preparation: 10 minutes

1/2 C. Alsatian vinaigrette (see recipe)
1 tbs. parsley
1 shallot, minced
1 garlic clove, minced
Pinch salt
Pinch pepper
1/4 tsp. chervil
3 C. emmental cheese, grated

1. Mix the vinaigrette, parsley, shallots, garlic, salt, pepper, and chervil.
2. Stir into the emmental cheese and serve.

Tips and suggestions:
Make this the same day you serve it.

Potato Salad

"Grombeere salad"

Salade de pommes de terre

Potatoes are king in Alsace. Cooked with crème fraîche and bacon, they are found as an accompaniment to almost every meal.

Preparation: 30 minutes

3 large potatoes
1/2 C. cubed bacon
1/2 C. Alsatian vinaigrette
(see recipe)
1 tbs. parsley
3 tbs. crème fraîche

1. Boil the potatoes in water for 20 minutes until the potatoes are tender and you can poke them easily with a fork. Peel the skins and let cool. Slice into disks about 1/2" thick.
2. Sautee the cubed bacon and save the fat.
3. Gently mix into the potatoes the vinaigrette, parsley, and crème fraiche, and top with the bacon and the warm bacon fat. Serve warm.

Tips and suggestions:
This should be made the same day and served warm.

Cervelas Sausage Salad

"Cervila salad"

Salade de cervelas

Cervelas is a thick traditional sausage whose taste reminds of baloney.

Preparation: 15 minutes
Marinade: 1 hour

1/2 C. Alsatian vinaigrette (see recipe)
1 tbs. parsley
1 shallot, minced
1 garlic clove, minced
Pinch salt
Pinch pepper
1/4 tsp. chervil
3 cervelas sausages
1 head of butter leaf lettuce
2 tomatoes

3 eggs, hard-boiled
1/8 tsp. salt
1/8 tsp. pepper
2 tbs. fromage blanc
1/2 tbs. parsley
1/4 tsp nutmeg

1. Mix the vinaigrette, parsley, shallot, garlic, salt, pepper, and chervil.

2. Slice the sausages in half lengthwise. On the round side, make small cuts with a knife for the marinade to soak in. Spread the vinaigrette mixture over the sausages. Marinate for at least an hour.

3. Prepare the egg garnish. Cut the hard-boiled eggs in half lengthwise and remove the yolks. Put the yolks in a bowl and mix with salt, pepper, fromage blanc, parsley, and nutmeg. Mix well and refill the egg whites. Sprinkle with paprika.

4. Arrange the lettuce on a serving tray and top with marinated sausages and quartered tomatoes. Sprinkle any leftover dressing over the tomatoes. Garnish with eggs.

Tips and suggestions:
The cervelas sausages may be prepared the night before serving. A bologna sausage may be used to replace the cervelas. Ricotta cheese may be used to replace the fromage blanc.

Cherry Tomato Cherry Salad

"Tomate salad met Kirsch"
Salade aux cerises et tomates

Although there are cherries in this recipe, this is not a dessert. Cherries are abundant in Alsace throughout the summer and are celebrated in many recipes.

"Solang ass d'r Kirschbaum bliejt, kann's noch Kirsch gann!"
As soon as the cherry tree blossoms, there is the hope of cherries!

Preparation: 10 minutes
Marinating: 30 minutes

1 C. cherry tomatoes
1 C. cherries
1 C. red grapes
Balsamic vinaigrette (see recipe)
2 tbs. fresh thyme

Tips and suggestions:
Fresh rosemary may be used to replace the thyme.

1. Slice cherry tomatoes, cherries, and grapes in half. Remove any seeds.
2. Toss with vinaigrette and fresh thyme. Let marinate for at least 1/2 hour before serving.

Foie Gras Tourt

"Fleischpastet"

Pâté en croûte

This is a traditional dish dating back to the nineteenth century. It is fairly expensive to make due to the goose liver and truffles, and therefore often reserved for special celebrations, such as marriages and baptisms.

Preparation: 30 minutes

Marinade: 8 hours

Baking: 50 minutes

1 lb. fresh goose liver

1/2 tsp. "four spices" (see recipe)

2 tsp. salt

1/2 C. kirsch

1/2 C. cognac

4 oz. veal filet

4 oz. pork filet

1/4 C. pistachios (optional)

1 tsp. olive oil

2 oz. black truffles

1 short crust pastry (see recipe)

1 egg white

1 egg yolk

1 gelatin sheet

1 C. veal stock

1/3 C. Madeira

Butter and flour to prepare the pan

1. Gently break the goose liver apart lengthwise and carefully remove any veins or membranes from the liver. (The butcher can do this for you.) Mix the four spices and salt together. Sprinkle the liver with half of this mixture. Marinate overnight in the kirsch and cognac.
2. Preheat the oven to 350°F. Butter and flour a loaf pan.
3. Mince the veal and pork, add the rest of the salt and four spices, and mix well. Toss with pistachios and olive oil.
4. Strain the liver. Slice the truffles and press into the surface of the liver.
5. Line the bottom and sides of the loaf pan with the short crust pastry. Be sure to save enough pastry to cover the top later.
6. Fill the bottom third of the pan with half of the pork and veal mixture. Place the liver pieces over the pork and veal mixture. Top the liver with the rest of the pork and veal mixture. Tap the pan well to remove any large air pockets.
7. Cover with the rest of the short crust pastry and seal the edges well, using the egg white to join the pastry. Cut two 1-inch circles in the top of the pastry crust and line each hole with a circle of extra pastry to make a sort of chimney. Brush the top of the pastry crust with the egg yolk.
8. Bake for 45 to 50 minutes. Insert a thin knife through the chimney to see if the center of the liver is warm. When the knife comes out warm remove the loaf from the oven and let cool.
9. While the loaf is cooking, soften the gelatin in warm water. Heat the veal stock and dissolve the softened gelatin into the stock. Remove from heat and stir in the Madeira. Pour this mixture into the chimneys after baking and it has almost cooled. If there is extra gelatin mixture, pour it over the top to seal the tourt. Cool in refrigerator overnight.
10. Slice and serve cold.

Tips and suggestions:
This should be finished the day before to let the flavors settle.
When choosing a goose liver, look for a slightly pink color with a firm smooth texture. Duck liver may be used to replace the goose liver.

Strawberries with Alsatian Cream

"Erdbeere met crème"

Fraises à la crème

Preparation: 10 minutes

6 C. strawberries
1 C. sugar
2 C. crème fraîche (see recipe)
1/4 C. schnapps
1/4 C. grilled hazelnuts

1. Slice the strawberries. Gently stir in sugar, crème fraîche, and schnapps. Keep cool.
2. Serve the strawberries in a bowl topped with whipped cream and hazelnuts.

Tips and suggestions:
Shortcakes or pound cake may be used to accompany this recipe instead of the hazelnut cake.
Make this the same day you serve it.

Hazelnut Tart

"Haselnussküeche"
Tarte aux noisettes

Preparation: 10 minutes
Baking: 1 hour

1 short crust pastry (see recipe)
4 eggs
1⅓ C. sugar
1/4 C. cream
2 tbs. kirsch
Pinch salt
1 tsp. vanilla
3½ C. ground hazelnuts
1/4 C. flour

Dry beans and wax paper

1. Preheat oven to 400°F. Butter and flour a tart pan and line with the short crust pastry. Cover pastry with wax paper and fill with dry beans to keep the shape of the crust stable. Pre-bake the crust for 15 minutes until it barely starts to color. Remove from the oven and cool. Lower the temperature to 350°F.

2. Mix the eggs and sugar well. Add the cream, kirsch, salt, and vanilla. Stir in the ground hazelnuts and flour. Pour into prebaked crust.

3. Bake for 40 to 50 minutes until golden brown. Remove from oven and let cool.

Tips and suggestions:
Almonds or walnuts may be used to replace the hazelnuts for this recipe. For the almonds, add a teaspoon of almond extract.
Hazelnut liquor may be used to replace the kirsch.

Add 1/2 C. flour for a more cake-like texture.

Branches

August

Radish Salad

Sautéed Frog Legs

Almond Trout

Alsatian Asparagus

Mirabelle Plum Pudding

Wine Suggestions
Pinot Gris or Riesling Wine

Covered Bridge

Old Man Féticke's Beautiful Legs

"Ich honn jo nit die Saue gehiet met dem."
I wouldn't leave my pigs with him. Or my frogs!

In the summertime, the canals that weave through Strasbourg are lined with people fishing. Old men have their favorite spots in the shade, and young boys emulate their fathers and cast, searching for the lazy trout swimming in the canals. It was August, and Ben invited Frederic and me to dinner to try some of the trout that he had caught in the countryside. We were eager to try more of his family recipes, and it was sure to be a pleasant evening. When we arrived at the door, Ben greeted us with his usual smile and kisses on the cheek, as well as with a glass of wine. As we chatted at the table with our wine, Ben placed an odd-looking appetizer on the table and encouraged us to try it. I hesitated to get a better look, while Frederic dug right in, exclaiming how delicious it was. "What is it?" I asked, trying to sound as polite as possible. Ben laughed at me and said, "Oh, you will not like it! You have been raised on frozen, plastic-wrapped chicken breasts. They are little frog legs, but try them anyway. They are good if you don't think about it. Like snails. It is an old family recipe." I was trapped. I was being served the very thing that my brothers used to chase me down the road with. Apparently, in Alsace, if one tried to frighten the girls by dangling frogs under their noses, they would probably collect the frogs with a "thank you," take them straight to the kitchen, fry them in butter, and eat them. I noticed that Frederic had slowed his consumption for a moment, but he soon overcame the idea of what he was eating. He was no help to me when he said, "Come on and try them. You eat chickens; they are just as ugly." I managed to nibble on one and it was truly mouth watering, but I kept thinking that I would later make the recipe with strips of chicken breasts and that would be good, too.

Over dinner Ben talked about his frog-hunting days. The ones we had eaten were from the frozen section of the grocery store, but when he was young, Ben was sent by his mother to catch frogs with the usual warning to watch out for the Hockemann. The infamous Hockmann was a devious character in Alsatian folklore with a large hook used to drag unwary victims to the bottom of his pond, where he would drown them. Was this a real monster, or a mythic character invented by mothers to convince children to stay away from dangerous water holes? How can we ever really know? Either way, the highly toned thighs of these little green jumpers were a favorite of the family, and Ben would meet his friends at the ponds—friends who also had the same missions and warnings and various tales and legends to share. What a dream for young boys to be actually sent by their mothers to chase frogs. There were many frogs and many young boys chasing them, so the competition was sometimes fierce, except for one pond—the largest and most beautiful pond in the village. It was filled with countless hopping shapely frogs and no little boys to chase them. Ben and his friends dreamed of going there, but one small obstacle stood in way of their dreams of glory and adventure—Monsieur Féticke, the owner of the pond. He was a large, muscular man with an enormous eyebrow—one eyebrow—which darkened his two eyes simultaneously and which he shaved to size periodically. M. Féticke, in addition to these impressionable attributes, also had a wooden hand that terrorized the young boys. It created a great deal of suspicion among the frog hunters. Could M. Féticke be the Hockemann incognito? Could this man whom all their mothers talked about at the market have fooled them into thinking he was someone else? Could their unsuspecting fathers be sure he was safe to drink beers with? Could M. Féticke attach a hook in place of his false hand and easily send young frog hunters to the bottom of the pond? In light of this logic, Ben and his friends naturally hunted for frogs in other village ponds, but the harvest wasn't as good as what he imagined possible in Féticke's pond.

One Friday when Ben was ten years old, his mother told him "Ben, this evening we are having frog legs and we will need a lot because your uncle is coming to dinner." A lot of frog legs were difficult. Very difficult. He hadn't planned for this. It would take a lot of time, and his friends would be long gone and the day over by the time he finished. Ben was desperate to find a shortcut, and he began to ponder the possibility of sneaking over to M. Féticke's pond. After some strategizing and images of pride in declaring his courage to his friends, he slipped along the fence, trying to concentrate on lovely frog thighs soaked in butter and garlic, instead of hooks and ominous eyebrows. This gave him the nerve to slide under the fence and quickly sprint to the pond. He plunged his net into the water while keeping an eye out for M. Féticke. There were more frogs that he had ever seen before. It was like a frog resort, and they were swimming and sunning themselves with no unease or fear caused by Ben's presence. Somewhere between greed and wonder, he lost sight of anything other than frogs until suddenly, M. Féticke's reflection appeared in the pond water. He froze with fear. It was true! Old man Féticke lived in his pond, just like Hockemann, and was going to thrust him down and drown him with his hook-hand. Old man Féticke grabbed his shoulder and asked him, *"Was machst du?* What are you doing, boy?"* Ben let out a cry and his flight instincts took control. He started running—running the fastest sprint of his young life—running with such effort that he surely made 100m in less than ten seconds. And as he ran, he pled to God to help him escape, promising to never again eat frog legs, never, never, ever, he promised. All the running and pleading paid off because just then Ben reached his house. Out of breath, he quickly dashed inside, gasping for air as he closed the door behind him. He loosened the vice of his grip on the bag and handed it to his mother while babbling something about Hockemann and M. Féticke. Despite the fear and the sprinting, he had not dropped the bag of frogs. At dinner, by which time he had collected himself, the frog legs had an unusually good aroma. As he watched his uncle devouring one leg after another, Ben thought that God wouldn't mind if he just tasted a few. As he licked the delicate bone of his first thigh, there was a knock at the door. It was old man Féticke.

Sautéed Frog Legs

"Froscheschenkel"
Cuisses de grenouilles

Fresh frogs are found in abundance in Alsace. Gourmet monks were plentiful as well. Therefore it is no surprise that they needed to be creative on Fridays and certain religious holidays when they weren't allowed to eat meat. To add variety, they developed recipes using frog legs and snails, which are categorized as fish instead of meat. They were evidently quite talented in cooking these little legs, as the tradition is still practiced today. The fresher the better! Smaller frogs are tastier that larger frogs.

Preparation Time: 10 minutes
Cooking time: 15 minutes

30 frog legs
2 shallots, minced
3 large garlic cloves, minced
1 egg yolk
1/4 C. butter
1/4 C. Pinot Blanc wine
1/4 C. parsley
2 tbs. crème fraîche (see recipe)
2 tbs. flour
1 tbs. lemon juice
1 tsp. grape seed oil
1/8 tsp. Worcestershire sauce
1/8 tsp. salt
Pinch of pepper
Pinch of nutmeg

1. Melt the butter and oil in saucepan over low heat. Add the shallots and garlic and sauté until soft. Remove the shallots and garlic from the pan and save for later.

2. Whip the egg yolk and lemon juice until it is light yellow. Mix the salt and flour in a separate bowl. Dip the frog legs in the egg yolk mixture, shake and repeat with the flour.

3. Increase the heat and let the butter brown lightly. Add pepper and nutmeg. Brown the frog legs quickly on both sides. Do not overcook.

4. Remove the frog legs and return the garlic and shallots to the pan. Add wine and reduce the volume by half over medium heat.

5. Lower the temperature and stir in the crème fraîche and parsley. Add the frog legs and sauté for 1 to 2 minutes while coating with the sauce.

6. Serve immediately.

Tips and suggestions:
If you can't quite make the leap to frog legs, feel free to substitute thin strips of chicken breast, calamari, shrimp, or mushrooms. Any dry white wine may be used.

Almond Trout, Alsatian Asparagus, Sautéed Frog Legs

Radish Salad

"Rettichsalat"
Salade de radis

This is an excellent entrée for frog legs.

Preparation: 10 minutes

About 30 radishes
12 slices of rye bread
2 tbs. butter
1 tbs. salt

Tips and suggestions:
Fromage blanc or cream cheese may be substituted for the butter.

1. Butter the bread slices and arrange on serving platter with the radishes and a small bowl of salt for dipping.

Almond Trout

"Forelle mit Mandeln"

Truites aux amandes

Alsace is between the Rhine River and the Vosges Mountains. There are many man-made canals as well as natural rivers running through the countryside and cities. Trout is plentiful and so are the recipes, including this one which is one of the most flavorful dishes of Alsace.

Preparation: 10 minutes
Cooking: 20 minutes

3 tbs. olive oil
6 trout filets
1 lemon, quartered
2 branches of thyme
2 bay leaves
1/4 C. parsley
1 tsp. sea salt
1 tbs. water
2 tsp. lemon juice
2 tsp. balsamic vinegar
1/2 C. toasted sliced almonds
3 tbs. butter

1. Preheat the oven to 400°F. Cover the bottom of a baking pan with olive oil. Place the trout skin side down in the pan. Add the quartered lemon, thyme, bay leaves, and parsley, and sprinkle the salt over the trout.

2. Bake in oven for 15 to 20 minutes, depending on the size of the trout filets.

3. After 10 minutes, add water to the pan. Sprinkle lemon juice and balsamic vinegar over the trout and continue baking until the flesh is firm and flaky.

4. Sauté almonds in butter until golden and sprinkle almonds over the top of the trout to serve.

Tips and suggestions:
Other fish may be substituted for the trout, such as perch, bass, salmon, and pike fish.

Alsatian Asparagus

"Sparischle met drei sauce"

Asperges aux trois sauces

In 1873, Pastor Heyler brought asparagus from his home in Algeria and planted it in Hoerdt, Alsace. Alsatians were quick to appreciate this vegetable that serves as a symbol of spring. In May, it is celebrated with a festival in the town of Village-Neuf. This recipe is traditionally served with Jambon Vigneron, a ham that is marinated in wine and then boiled. However, the almond trout is delicious with this recipe as well.

Preparation: 5 minutes
Cooking: 15 minutes

1 cube of chicken broth
Pinch of salt
2 bunches white asparagus
String

Condiments:
Mayonaise (see recipe)
Dijon vinaigrette (see recipe)
Mousseline sauce (see recipe)

1. Boil water with salt and cube of chicken broth.
2. Peel the base of the asparagus and tie into bundles of about 6. Place in boiling water with their tips pointed upward and above the water line. Cook for about 15 minutes until a fork can pierce the stalks.
3. Remove from boiling water and place directly into a bowl of ice water for 30 seconds to stop the cooking. Remove and drain on towel.
4. Serve along with the three sauces as condiments.

Tips and suggestions:
Green asparagus may be used in this recipe as well. The condiments may be purchased to save time.

Mirabelle Plum Pudding

"Mirabelle oflaf"

Gratin de mirabelles

Mirabelles are cultivated in Alsace and even more so in its neighboring province, Lorraine. The mirabelle is a small golden plum and is used in tarts, jams, puddings, sorbets, and, of course, schnapps. Each year in Ben's hometown there is a Mirabelle Queen, who presides over their Mirabelle Festival in August.

Preparation: 15 minutes
Marinade: 8 hours
Cooking: 20 minutes

4 C. mirabelle plums
1/2 C. mirabelle schnapps
1 tbs. powdered sugar
2 eggs
1 egg yolk
1/4 C. sugar
1/4 tsp. vanilla
1/4 C. half and half
1/4 C. flour
1/4 C. ground hazelnuts
2 tbs. sugar
Pinch of salt
2 tbs. cold butter
1 egg white

Butter for pan
Schnapps for flambé (optional)
Ice cream (optional)

1. Marinate mirabelle plums in the schnapps and powdered sugar overnight.

2. Butter 6 individual ramekins. Preheat the oven to 350°F. Place the rack on the top level.

3. Strain and divide the mirabelles into individual ramekin dishes.

4. Mix the whole eggs, egg yolk, and 1/4 cup of sugar. Add the liquid from the marinade and whisk over a double boiler until the cream turns foamy and thickens. Remove from heat and add vanilla and half and half.

5. Mix flour, ground hazelnuts, 2 tbs. sugar, and salt in a bowl. Cut in cold butter, forming a crumbly mixture. Whisk egg white until foamy and stir into the crumb mixture. Sprinkle over the mirabelles.

6. Bake in oven for 15 to 20 minutes until golden. At the table, pour a teaspoon of schnapps over the top and flambé.

7. Serve cold or warm with a scoop of ice cream (vanilla or mint), coffee with schnapps, or green walnut liquor.

Tips and suggestions:
You may replace the mirabelles with cherries, blueberries, or raspberries. You may replace the hazelnuts with almonds. If you can't find them powdered you can powder them in a clean coffee grinder, but be careful not to turn them into nut butter.
The mirabelle schnapps may be replaced with a fruit brandy, port, or cognac.
Green walnut liquor is also an excellent replacement for the schnapps if you have the time to make it or if you can find it in you local liquor store. It tastes like a spiced tawny port.

Col de bavelle

September

Alsatian Sauerkraut

Raw Sauerkraut

Liver Dumplings

Country Potatoes

Munster Cheese with Cumin

Raisin and Almond Cake

Wine and Beer Suggestions
Meal—Riesling Wine or Blond Beer
Dessert—Coffee with Schnapps

The Sauerkraut Cabin

"Ich ess alles gar user Surkrutt das ess ich sehr gar."
I like everything except sauerkraut, that, I adore.

Sauerkraut is a dish of fermented cabbage, which is to say cabbage that has been left a little too long in its corner. Before the invention of the refrigerator, fermentation made it possible to preserve cabbage in order to keep a supply of the vegetable during the winter or on long voyages. Cabbage is rich in vitamin C and nutrients, which allowed Christopher Columbus to nourish his sailors while avoiding the scurvy, and therefore is indirectly responsible for the discovery of the New World! The origin of this recipe is lost in the midst of time, but possibly comes from China. Perhaps it came to Europe in the luggage of the hordes of Genghis Khan. One could say that it is a meal of adventure. While making its way across Europe to people of Alsace, various ingredients were added to the original recipe until the Alsatians had the luminous idea of adding Riesling wine to the simmering cabbage. This added a note of delicacy and refinement to the dish. For those lucky enough to be in Alsace in September, there is a sauerkraut festival as well as a sauerkraut route that winds through the cabbage fields in the countryside with stops for tasting.

I have an Austrian grandmother and therefore memories of cabbage boiling in the kitchen. The passion never rubbed off on me until Frederic and I went to a traditional restaurant in Strasbourg known for its sauerkraut. What had I been missing! How could I have been so blind? It was addictive. I craved it for days while listening to Frederic's stomach still digesting a healthy portion. Without delay, I bought some raw sauerkraut at the Saturday market and asked Ben to teach me how to cook it. We made two kilograms, about four pounds, worth of sauerkraut and finished it in two days! Ben was a master of the dish and while I took notes, he weaved in stories of growing up with sauerkraut and M. Stubber, a man from his village, famous—or infamous—for his love of the boiled cabbage.

Beginning early in their youth, Alsatian stomachs are subjected to a rigorous daily training consisting of "light" delicacies such as meat pies, Baekoeffe, sausages, and potatoes, etc., which gives them, in majority, the capacity to easily digest a plate of sauerkraut loaded with anything pork. But nature has a way of throwing curve balls to some people, and now and then Alsace produces certain individuals who are not cut out for the rigors of sauerkraut. To be unable to digest a plate of sauerkraut is a great tragedy in Alsace, but worse still is to be unable to digest it while having a passionate love for it. This is an impossible situation that often leads to ostracism. Compassion and tolerance should be given to these poor souls.

M. Stubber was of this unfortunate condition. He was a forest ranger, a healthy, large, strapping man, with the makings of a movie star. But a different kind of stardom was to be M. Stubber's destiny; he was a sauerkraut lover who had the plighted misfortune of being unable to digest it without unpleasant side effects. These side effects appeared in gaseous form and with such generosity that they undoubtedly contributed to global warming. There were only two ways to handle the problem: Give up the beloved sauerkraut, or live alone in a cabin outside of the village. He naturally chose the latter and lived in the forest with his dog, Chou, where he could indulge unabashedly in his passion for sauerkraut. He ate his favorite dish each day that the good Lord gave him. If one had the courage to visit him there, one would see a large cauldron sitting on an old wood fire stove in which bubbled enough sauerkraut to support a long siege. M. Stubber never completely emptied his cauldron, but instead, added cabbage after each meal, bringing it back to the original level. It was whispered in the village that the cauldron was inherited and had never been emptied since its first day in the Stubber family.

Ben knew M. Stubber well and would often cut wood for him to earn money. The wood was needed to feed the stove where the sauerkraut pot bubbled day and night. Ben really needed the money at this time, and the whole house was filled with the sauerkraut fumes, thanks to the wood Ben chopped so diligently. The odor penetrated the walls. But there were more odors than those of boiling cabbage, given M. Stubber's propensity for flatulence. Good thing that he did not smoke. Compounding the situation was his insistence on keeping the windows closed in order to save on the heating bill. After Ben chopped a pile of wood, M. Stubber always invited him to come inside and have a plate of sauerkraut before going home. It was hard to resist because M. Stubber was, after all, a sauerkraut aficionado and Ben picked up many tips over time. At the table, this kind man, in light of his daily contact with nature, found no shame in bodily functions. If he felt the need to relieve himself of gas after having eaten a good sauerkraut, he did. After all, it isn't healthy to hold back one's natural gases, that was his life philosophy. He had thus taken to the habit of letting his intestines speak out during any occasion, public or not, without feeling the least bit of embarrassment, and this was sometimes quite a monologue. The monologue often turned into a duet as Chou participated from under the table. Poor Chou was also nourished with healthy doses of sauerkraut and, alas, suffered from the same torments as his master. But all this suffering was nothing in comparison to the pleasure and profound satisfaction that M. Stubber found at the table with his sauerkraut. He was not a very religious man, but he had the feeling of a sacred union that passed between him and his sauerkraut. In the evening when he added two good sausages and a cut of ham to his steaming bowl of cabbage, he felt there was meaning to his life and the world was safeguarded for one more day.

Night Musings

Alsatian Sauerkraut, Liver Dumplings, and Country Potatoes

Alsatian Sauerkraut

"Surkrut"
Choucroute à l'Alsacienne

This dish has evolved in Alsace from a simple way to preserve a vegetable for the winter months into a gastronomic celebration. The countryside is dotted with cabbage farms and a sauerkraut route that winds through the countryside just like the famous wine route. This dish is loved and revered among Alsatians. Riesling and pork remain essential ingredients, but the spices have varied over time, including cumin, elderberry, and dill. Today, juniper berries are the spice of choice and add a delicious flavor to the mix.

Preparation Time: 30 min.
Cooking time: 2 h 30 min.

4 lbs. raw sauerkraut (see recipe)
5 liters of boiling water
1 tbs. white wine vinegar
2 whole yellow onions
2 garlic cloves
12 whole cloves
1/4 C. of butter
1 bottle of Riesling
3 bay leaves
8 juniper berries
1 sprig of thyme
1 carrot
Sea salt to taste
1/4 tsp. white pepper
Pinch of coriander

1 pig knuckle or ½ lb. smoked pork shoulder
1-inch thick or 3 thick slices smoked bacon
1-inch thick slice unsmoked bacon
3 thick slices ham
6 knacks or hotdogs
4 Strasbourg sausages or bratwursts
2 cervelas or bologne sausages

Condiments:
Pommes de Terre Roties
9 liverwurst quenelles
Horseradish sauce (see recipe)
Dijon mustard

1. Rinse the sauerkraut in cold water. Boil water with white wine vinegar and wash the sauerkraut in the boiling water for 5 minutes. Drain.

2. Peel and spear onions and garlic with the whole cloves. In a large kettle, sauté in butter over low heat for 2 minutes. Don't brown the butter.

3. Add half of the sauerkraut and 1/2 bottle of Riesling to the pot. Add bay leaves, juniper berries, thyme, carrot, salt, pepper, and coriander. Cover with the rest of the sauerkraut. Place the lid on the pot and simmer for 1½ hours, stirring occasionally and adding wine occasionally to keep a layer of liquid in the pan.

4. Pierce the sausages a few times with a knife. Add all the pork except the bratwurst. Cover and simmer, while stirring occasionally.

5. Remove the bacon and set aside when it is cooked. Add the remaining wine; cover and continue to simmer until no more liquid is in the pot, about 2 hours.

6. During this time, fry bratwurst in pan and prepare condiments.

7. Remove onions from sauerkraut and cut in half. Add any oil or butter from the bratwurst, liver dumplings, and potatoes to the sauerkraut.

8. Pile the sauerkraut in the center of a large serving plate in the shape of a mound. Decorate the mound of sauerkraut with onions, garlic, and pork, including the bratwurst and liver dumplings.

Tips and suggestions:
You may cook this the day before except for the bratwurst and quenelles. Reheating the next day brings out even more flavor. The Riesling may be replaced with a dry white wine. The meat should be a variety of pork, but you may change the type according to taste. Be sure to include smoked bacon.

I recommend buying raw sauerkraut if you can find it. It is generally inexpensive and saves a lot of time. However, if you would like to make your own, a recipe is included at the end of this chapter. Make sure that the cabbage is sliced very thin.

Liver Dumplings

"Lewerknephle"
Quenelles de foie

This dish is of German origin. In fact, the king of Bavaria kept an Alsatian woman at court by the name of Madame Kayser. She was an expert in preparing these dumplings. It is often served with fried onions and croutons, along with a salad or with the beloved sauerkraut.

Preparation: 15 minutes
Refrigeration: 1 hour
Cooking: 20 minutes

1/2 lb. pork liver
1/4 lb. smoked bacon
1 onion
1 garlic clove
1 tbs. fresh parsley
1/2 C. breadcrumbs
1/2 C. milk
2 eggs
1/4 C. flour
1/4 tsp. salt
1/8 tsp. pepper
1/8 tsp. nutmeg
2 tbs. butter
1 small onion, sliced

1. Mince the liver, bacon, onion, garlic, and parsley by passing through a grinder.
2. Soak the breadcrumbs in milk and drain. Mix with ground meat, flour, salt, pepper, and nutmeg. Beat the eggs and mix into the ground meat as well. Refrigerate for 1 hour.
3. Shape into dumplings the size of a small egg. Poach in simmering hot salted water for about 10 minutes. The dumplings are done when they rise to the top. Remove and drain.
4. Before serving, sauté the sliced onion in butter over low heat until transparent. Add dumplings and continue to sauté for 5 minutes.
5. Serve warm.

Tips and suggestions:
After poaching the quenelles, the water can serve as an excellent broth. Just add parsley, noodles, and a few carrots, and you have a soup for the next day. Beef liver may also be used for this recipe.
To save time, buy prepared liver dumplings and sauté in the butter and onions before serving.

Country Potatoes

"Grumbeere"

Pommes paysannes

Potatoes were originally misunderstood in Alsace. They were used to feed the pigs, the noble creatures of Alsace, and they are commonly referred to as "devil's fruit" due to their odd shape and lack of color. Today they are honored in many recipes and even claim a place on the same platter as the esteemed sauerkraut.

"Ohne Grumbeere hat mer jo nit gess."

Without potatoes on the menu, one has not really eaten.

Preparation: 5 minutes
Cooking: 25 minutes

6 medium firm potatoes
2 tbs. butter
3 tbs. vegetable oil
1 onion, sliced
Pinch salt
Pinch nutmeg

1. Preheat oven to 400°F.
2. Slice the potatoes into thirds. Sauté over medium heat with butter, oil, salt, and onions until golden.
3. Sprinkle with nutmeg and place in oven for 15 minutes.

Tips and suggestions:
Include the butter from the liver dumplings to fry the country potatoes and add the same butter to the sauerkraut before serving.

Munster Cheese with Cumin

"Munsterkäs met Kummel"
Fromage de Munster au cumin

Irish Benedictine monks living in Munster Valley during the thirteenth century developed Munster cheese. The cheese grew in popularity throughout Alsace and took the name of Munster, which means monastery. During the fifteenth century, spices were traveling through Alsace along the trade routes. Among the spices were cumin and star anise, with which many Alsatians began to season their Munster. Today, Munster with cumin is still a common combination.

"Ces Fromages dont l'aspect fait d'abord horreur, sont si délicieux qu'on les mange sur la table des grandes seigneurs"—
Benedictin Dom Tailly
"These cheese of which the initial scent is horrifying, are so delicious that one eats them at the table of great noblemen."

Preparation: 5 minutes

1 round of Munster cheese
1/2 tsp. whole cumin
6 slices of five-grain bread

1. Slice the Munster round into 12 triangles
2. Slightly roast the cumin in a saucepan over low heat until you can smell the spice readily.
3. Sprinkle cumin over the Munster slices and serve with the five-grain bread.

Tips and suggestions:
You may replace the Munster with another cheese, such as pecorino, tome, cheddar, or even a goat cheese, according to your tastes. The bread may also be replaced by a dark grain or pumpernickel bread.

Kougelhopf Traditions

Raisin and Almond Bread

"Kougelhopf"
Kougelhopf

The Kougelhopf is a specialty in Alsace that has its own ceramic baking dish similar in shape to a Bundt pan. It is a brioche-style bread most likely of Austrian origin, and it spread throughout Alsace at the time of Marie-Antoinette. Traditionally, villagers brought their own milk, butter, eggs, schnapps, and ceramic mold to the bakery. The baker would provide the flour, sugar, raisins, almonds, yeast, and elbow grease. Later in the day the villagers would pick up their baked kougelhopf. This tradition continued until World War II; however, there are still a few villages that continue this tradition today. There is also a savory version with walnuts and bacon that dates back to the nineteenth century that was rediscovered in recent years. Both versions are readily found in bakeries around Alsace.

Preparation: 2 hours
Marinade: 8 hours
Cooking: 45 minutes

1/2 C. raisins
2 tbs. kirsch
1 C. milk
1/4 C. sugar
1 tbs. dry yeast
1/2 C. butter
2 eggs
1/4 tsp. salt
3 C. flour

About 25 whole almonds
1/4 C. powdered sugar

Ceramic kougelhopf mold
or Bundt pan
Butter and flour to
prepare the pan

1. Marinate the raisins in kirsch overnight.
2. Heat the milk gently in saucepan until it is lukewarm. Place half of the milk in a small bowl and stir in 1 tbs. sugar. Add yeast. Let stand in warm place for 10 minutes until mixture doubles.
3. In a large mixing bowl, cream butter with the remaining sugar. Mix in the remaining milk, eggs, and salt. Add the yeast mixture and incorporate the flour.
4. Place dough on floured surface and knead by hand for 15 minutes. Cover with a cheesecloth and set in warm place to rise for 1 hour.
5. Butter and flour a 9-inch Bundt pan. Place almonds into the grooves at the bottom of the pan, making a nice pattern.
6. Incorporate the raisins into the dough. Work the dough into a circle and make a whole in the center. Place dough into the prepared Bundt pan and press down slightly. Cover with a cheesecloth and set in warm place until the dough rises one inch from the top of the pan.
7. Preheat oven to 325 °F.
8. Bake in oven for 45 minutes until golden brown. Cool upside down on wire rack. Remove from pan and sprinkle with powdered sugar to serve.

Tips and suggestions:
Before serving, a shot of kirsch or other brandy may be poured over each slice.
To make the savory version, simply reduce the sugar to 1 tbs. and replace the raisins with smoked bacon and replace the almonds with walnuts.

Raw Sauerkraut

"Rëjes Surkrut"
Choucroute crue

The word "Surkrut" has German origin and literally means sour cabbage. In Alsace, other vegetables are preserved in the same way for the winter month, including the popular turnip. It is important to slice the vegetables thinly.

Preparation: 30 minutes
Fermentation: 3 weeks

Wood or ceramic barrel

Enough green cabbage to fill barrel
1 lb. sea salt
5 juniper berries

1. Remove the green cabbage leaves and slice the white part of the cabbage as thin as possible. Layer the green leaves in the bottom of the barrel.
2. Layer an inch of sliced cabbage and cover with sea salt. Repeat these layers until the barrel is full. Finish with a handful of sea salt and the juniper berries and cover with a cheesecloth and lid that can sink into the barrel. Place a large rock or brick on the lid to weigh it down.
3. The next day, the lid should be submerged in liquid. Let the cabbage ferment for 3 weeks, adding water to cover the cabbage as needed.

Tips and suggestions:
The longer the cabbage ages, the more bitter it will taste. Washing it well before using should take care of the bitter taste.
This method may be applied to turnips and fennel as well.

Mountains

October

New Wine and Fresh Cream Cheese

Onion Tart

Devil's Ham

Creamed Pumpkin

Watercress Salad

Blueberry Tart

Wine Suggestions
Appetizers—Vin Borru (New Wine) or Cider
Meal—Pinot Noir, Beaujolais, or Dark Beer
Dessert—Coffee with Cherry Schnapps

Cathedral

The Gourmet Ghost

"Gut esse un trinke Halt Leib un Seel zomme!"
Eating and drinking well keeps body and soul together!

D'Schlosserstub is an old tavern that once served as a gathering place for the members of the guild of key and lock makers. The ancient beer hall is large and dark, the ceiling is low, the clouds of smoke are opaque, the tables are carved out of wood, and the glasses of beer are deep. Ben and I were sitting in a corner with our beers. "Mince! It is not so easy being a pâtissier sometimes. I'm not just talking about starting at the bottom rung and working your way up to a place where skill is recognized. That was not always pleasant, but the worst was working in an old secluded manor where strange things happened." I had to interrupt, "Ben, you have worked in castles and manors! How exciting! I have often wondered what it is like to live in magnificent places like that." "Mais non, Susan, it is beautiful, yes, but those places have a history you know." Raising his second glass of beer to make a toast, Ben looked me right in the eyes over the edge of his glass and whispered, "I'm going to tell you a story you will not believe, the story of the merchant phantom." Now Ben can be superstitious at times, so I didn't take the ghost story seriously right away. I had already heard him explain a broken wine glass as possible ghost activity. I figured that he heard the locals recount various legends, which he took more seriously that I might. "Ben, you don't really believe in ghosts, do you?" I challenged. Not a good idea. He only grew uneasier and waived his hand about saying, "Mais oui! Everyone knows there are ghosts!" I could see beads of sweat forming on this forehead as he continued, "I have seen a ghost and it is something that I can't forget, the memory of it drives me out of my home to wander the streets certain evenings." He lowered his voice, "I will tell you the story and you can decide if you believe it."

He took a long drink from his beer as I moved my chair in closer. Then he began. "Not long ago, a friend of mine who was a head chef at a country inn in the beautiful Vosges Mountains was moving to Mulhouse to open his own restaurant and recommended me to take his place. What a chance to live in the mountains where the air was brisk, crème frâiche was available from the neighboring farms, and it still snowed in the winters. It was a rustic inn where visitors seeking a refuge from city life could escape for a few days, and we served them unforgettable meals and tucked them into feather beds at night. The inn was an old half-timbered farmhouse, a weathered Alsatian home that had belonged to a wealthy merchant in the eighteenth century.

"I was looking forward to a peaceful life at the inn. It had been a few weeks since I arrived. I quickly met the neighbors from the surrounding farms and greeted them as I passed by in the mornings to purchase fresh eggs, cream, and vegetables at the market. My boss was sensible and did not interfere as I prepared my Riesling tortes, sauerkrauts, quiches, tartes, and pastries. It was better than I had expected, and then things started happening: my fresh cream spoiled, my pots of whipped cream deflated when I looked away, I burned my tarts, my bottles of Gewurztraminer and kirsch disappeared, and my sauerkraut wouldn't ferment. I scrutinized the kitchen apprentices and staff, but it was impossible to find them at fault. Meanwhile, I had a difficult time explaining the abnormal consumption of wine and kirsch to the owner, who, in turn, began supervising me more closely. I became increasingly nervous; I doubted my abilities. I thought that perhaps I was not made for this pitiless kitchen trade after all. Then, one day I went to the cellar to fetch a ham. When I got to the bottom of the steps, the door slammed shut and the lights went out. I felt something rub against my arm, something cold and dry. I was petrified. I dropped the ham and screamed. I ran up the stairs and banged on the door until someone heard me and let me out. It had been locked from the outside. I told my boss that I had a family emergency, got in my car and left the inn quickly. Very quickly. I went to see my friend, the former head chef and I told him everything. ' Ohh la la,' he said shaking his head, 'I forgot to tell you. Let me explain, it is very simple. The inn once belonged to a rich grocer who moved there with his ravishing new bride and some servants, one of whom was a dashing young cook. The young bride fell in love with the cook instead of her new husband and soon began a torrid affair. The merchant found them out and died most suddenly. Was his death brought about by a broken heart—or by poison? Rumors abound. The cook soon married the young widow of the unfortunate grocer. It is said that the phantom of the grocer has taken out his revenge on cooks ever since.' My friend's advice? 'Make him a good blueberry tart from time to time (the merchant was a gourmet after all) and pair it with a glass of kirsch, put all this in the cellar and you will see, the phantom will leave you alone. No problem.'" Ben shuddered as he called to the waiter for another beer.

New Wine and Fresh Cream Cheese

"Nejer met bibelskäs"
Vin bourru et fromage blanc

Vin bourru is wine that has just begun the fermentation process. You can buy this at the markets for only a couple of weeks and then it disappears until the next harvest. It is as if one can't wait to taste the year's new wine and celebrate the harvest. It is sweet, unclarified, has a low alcohol content, and has a strong white grape juice flavor. There are also fromage blanc festivals at this time, and the two products go well together.

Preparation: 5 minutes

1/3 C. crème fraîche (see recipe)
2 C. fromage blanc (see Fresh Cream Cheese recipe)
1/4 tsp. salt
1/8 tsp. pepper
1/2 tsp. nutmeg
12 slices of walnut bread
3 tbs. chives, chopped
1/2 C. whole walnuts
1 bottle vin bourru

1. Mix crème fraîche and fromage blanc. Stir in salt, pepper, and nutmeg. Spread on the slices of bread. Sprinkle the chives over the top and slightly press the walnuts onto the cream mixture.

2. Serve with vin bourru.

Tips and suggestions:
You may replace the vin bourru with white grape juice, fresh apple cider, or hard cider. Some vineyards in the US sell unfermented grape juice from their harvest. Cream cheese or ricotta may be used to replace the fromage blanc.

New Wine and Fresh Cream Cheese, Onion Tart

Onion Tart

"Zeewelkueche"
Tarte à l'oignon

This dish is a close relative of the better known quiche.

Preparation: 10 minutes
Baking: 30 minutes

1 puff pastry
6 large yellow onions
1/2 tsp. salt
1/2 tsp. pepper
1/2 tsp. nutmeg
1 tbs. butter
1/2 tbs. flour
1 egg yolk
2 tbs. milk
1/2 C. crème fraîche (see recipe)
1 tbs. cubed bacon

1. Preheat the oven to 400°F. Line tart pan with wax paper and puff pastry. Poke holes in the pastry crust.
2. Slice onions thinly. In a covered frying pan, sauté onions, salt, pepper, and nutmeg in butter over low heat until transparent. Add flour and sauté for 1 minute without browning the flour. Cool.
3. Mix egg yolk, milk, and crème fraiche. Stir in the onion mixture. Pour into tart pan and sprinkle bacon over the top.
4. Bake in oven for 30 minutes until the pastry is golden. Cover with another sheet of wax paper if the bacon begins to burn.
5. Serve warm.

Tips and suggestions:
Fromage blanc may be used to replace the crème fraîche to create a lighter taste.

Devil's Ham, Creamed Pumpkin, Watercress Salad

Devil's Ham

"Schiefala"
Pallette à la diable

Preparation: 10 minutes
Baking: 1 hour 5 minutes

2 lb. boiled ham
2/3 C. whole grain Dijon mustard
2/3 C. Dijon mustard
1/2 tsp. salt
1/2 tsp. pepper
1 garlic clove mashed
1 tbs. parsley
1/2 C. smoked bacon cubes
1 C. dark beer

1. Preheat oven to 400°F.
2. Place ham in a ceramic baking dish. Mix the mustards, salt, pepper, garlic, and parsley and spread over the entire ham. Place bacon in the baking dish around the ham.
3. Bake in oven for 50 minutes. Increase the temperature to 475°F and add beer to the baking dish. Bake for another 15 minutes. The mustard crust should brown well, but if it starts to burn, cover with a piece of wax paper.

Tips and suggestions:
Use a dark brown beer in this recipe.
This dish is also made with horseradish and cream in place of the mustard.
This ham is good for cold meat sandwiches the next day.

Watercress Salad

"Rebkresse"
Salade de mâche

Preparation: 5 minutes

6 C. watercress salad
Nutmeg vinaigrette (see recipe)

1. Wash and dry the watercress. Toss with nutmeg vinaigrette.
2. Serve.

Creamed Pumpkin

"Gratinerter potimarron"

Gratin de potimarron

Potimarrons are sweet Chinese pumpkins.

Preparation: 10 minutes
Baking: 20 minutes

1 small pumpkin
1 onion
1/4 tsp. salt
1/8 tsp. pepper
1/2 tsp. nutmeg
1/2 C. crème fraîche (see recipe)
1 tbs. butter
2/3 C. breadcrumbs

Butter for the baking dish

1. Butter a ceramic baking dish well. Preheat the oven to 425°F.
2. Peel and remove the seeds from the pumpkin. Cut into small cubes and place in large bowl. Chop onion and add to pumpkin.
3. Stir in salt, pepper, nutmeg, and crème fraiche. Place in baking dish and dot with pieces of butter. Sprinkle the top with breadcrumbs.
4. Bake in oven for 20 minutes until the pumpkin pieces are soft and easily pierced with a fork. Serve warm.

Tips and suggestions:
Any pumpkin works well with this recipe as well. Sage and garlic may be added according to taste.

Blueberry Tart

"Heidelbeerekueche"

Tarte aux mytrilles

Aficionados will warn you that the North American blueberry is not the same as the European myrtille. Although outwardly similar in shape and color, blueberries are indigenous to North America, are generally much bigger, and have white pulp. Myrtilles grow wild throughout the Vosges Mountains, and blueberries are cultivated (they were imported from the US for that purpose). However, both varieties taste much the same.

Preparation: 10 minutes
Marinade: 8 hours
Baking: 40 minutes

1 C. sugar
1/4 C. schnapps
3 C. blueberries
Short crust pastry (see recipe)
1 tsp. sugar
1 tbs. cold butter
6 tbs. crème fraîche or vanilla ice cream

1. The night before, mix sugar, schnapps, and blueberries and let marinate in the refrigerator overnight.

2. Line tart pan with wax paper and short crust pastry. Poke holes in the pastry crust. Preheat the oven to 350°F.

3. Drain the blueberries and set aside the liquid. Fill tart pan with the blueberries. Sprinkle 1 tsp. of sugar over the blueberries.

4. Bake tart in oven for 30 to 40 minutes until the crust is golden. Cover with wax paper if the blueberries start to burn.

5. Reduce the blueberry liquid in a saucepan until it lines a wooden spoon.* Remove from heat and whisk in cold butter. Five minutes before the tart is done baking pour the sauce over the blueberries. Let finish cooking for the last 5 minutes.

6. Serve warm with crème fraiche or ice cream.

Tips and suggestions:
You may replace schnapps with brandy or Calvados. Frozen blueberries may be used for this as well.
* Lining a wooden spoon is a way to check the thickness of the sauce. Dip the wooden spoon in the sauce and run you finger across the back of the spoon. If the sauce holds the print from your finger mark, it is ready.

Street Musician and Child

November

Riesling Soup

Curried Endive Salad with Apples

Rabbit with Dijon Mustard Sauce

Mashed Carrots and Potatoes

Red Cabbage with Apples

Alsatian Cheese Tart

Caramelized Pears

Wine Suggestions
Soup and Salad—Gewürztraminer or Riesling Wine
Meal—Bordeaux or Côte-du-Rhône
Dessert—Mulled Wine with Schnapps

Grand-père and his Schnapps,
Photographed by Laurent Federlin

Schnapps

"Er schett's nit in d'Schueh"
He doesn't pour it in his shoes!
"Mer soll kinne e Au zudricke, un monschmol zwei."
One must know how to close an eye and sometimes two.

The French have long been possessed with the unshakable notion that alcohol, and wine in particular, possesses medicinal properties. Monasteries safeguarded the beer- and wine-making techniques introduced and developed by the Romans—along with Latin culture and literature. Monks were especially fervent believers in the medicinal properties of alcohol; most cloisters as well as some hospitals had at least one winery, brewery, or distillery. As late as the beginning of the twentieth century, manual workers were insured a minimum daily supply of red wine to keep up their strength. The French Army of World War I lacked weapons, canons, ammunition, food, boots, gas masks, and shelters to face the opposing German army, but one thing that French soldiers did not lack was wine. Two liters of red wine were included in the soldiers' daily rations and was thought partly responsible for the final victory. Today, alcohol in all its forms is produced in the region: fine beers, marvelous white wines, and various fruit brandies or schnapps. The varieties of schnapps that can be found testify to the abundant supply and diversity of fruits grown there: veille prune (aged prune), mirabelle, Pear Williams, quetsche, and the most famous, kirsch (cherry). Schnapps even enjoys the distinct honor of having its own glassware, the "stamperl." True schnapps are not sweetened like the schnapps found in the US. It is necessary to have a license to manufacture alcohol (a license that is often passed down from father to son), and the proof and law limit the quantities of alcohol manufactured each year. But of course, local distillers often interpret this law as a mere suggestion of quantities and degree and feel free to follow whatever the family recipe dictates (until they get caught).

Ben taught Frederic and me to appreciate fine schnapps. After hearing that I bought a bottle from the store to taste, Ben warned right away, "If you want to taste a real schnapps, you have to know a paysan. I know a farmer not too far from here that still makes the real thing. Don't tell Frederic, I will get a bottle and surprise him." He had known Frederic well enough by this time to realize how blissful this gift would make him. Ben showed up one evening with a confident smile and a used bottle of wine filled with a clear liquid. The bottle contained mirabelle schnapps of a quality that rivaled a carefully aged cognac. This nectar warmed our throats and stomachs while dissolving away our sluggishness after having a little too much for dinner that evening. As we appreciated our good fortune and fine friend, Ben spoke to us of his beloved grandfather and his love for the eau-de-vie.

"My grandfather taught me how to appreciate simple things in life: walks in the woods, an afternoon working in the garden, a slice of homemade bread with fresh butter. He was a true paysan. His hands always smelled of the soil from his garden. I have many memories of him. I can picture my grandpa taking me by the hand and saying, 'eh petit, taste this for me, it's very good,' as he passed to me the first apple of the year from his great wrinkled hands. He loved life in the country. When he wasn't working in his garden and orchards, he was preparing old recipes, and his favorite of all—schnapps."

Ben went on to describe his grandfather and his position in the village as a home distiller, in other words, a schnapps maker. Using a tested family recipe, he made his own schnapps from fruits gathered in the orchards and meadows nearby. Neighbors would also participate by bringing him their extra apples, quetsches, raspberries, pears, mirabelles, blueberries, and of course, cherries. In exchange, they received a percentage of the resulting schnapps. Sometimes Ben would help his grandfather in this noble endeavor and he remembers distilling his first bottle of schnapps at the age of nine. "It is time for you to learn a trade." Ben sat for hours watching the old metal distiller in the backyard percolate as small drops of a clear liquid seeped from the spout. It was a serious occasion as his grandfather directed Ben in the art of distilling fruit. Throughout the day, Ben would carry small samples to his grandfather sitting in a supervisory chair and wait for further instructions as his grandfather evaluated the development of the product. The first "coulée" that came out was put in special bottles to be used as friction alcohol for muscle sores. The best medicine there was! By the end of the day, they had a healthy supply of schnapps both in bottles and in grandpa. As a home distiller, Ben's grandfather took great pride in his final product and considered his schnapps a part of the food pyramid. It was an element as essential to his daily diet as bread and sausages. He had a theory that schnapps killed microbes, lowered cholesterol, increased intellectual performance, aided sound sleeping, improved the libido, and gave an overall sense of well-being and vitality. (This theory has not been completely verified.) Therefore, with much confidence, he put schnapps in his soup, soaked his bread in it, poured it over his meat like a white sauce, mixed it into his coffee, and included it in his strawberry tarts. He was known to hide a bottle under the dining table and quickly add some of its content to his meal when his suspicious wife turned her back. He had a large red nose, round cheeks, and a faint scent of schnapps wherever he went, yet he never seemed to be drunk. One would think that such a diet would kill a man within a few years, but not Ben's grandfather. He lived to the ripe old age of ninety-six and worked in his garden daily until the very end. Ben recalled the last day of his grandfather's life for Frederic and me. His grandpa had been taken to his bed after he had collapsed in the garden. The entire family was gathered around him. When the doctor arrived, he realized that his patient would not live through the night, and asked the dying patriarch if he would like something to ease his pain. "A stamperl of schnapps," replied Ben's grandfather in a frail voice. The doctor conceded, and Ben's grandmother brought him their finest kirsch in a crystal glass. He drank his shot with emotion and died immediately after. He had a smile on his face.

Riesling Soup

"Wisser winsupp"
Soupe au vin blanc

"S gibt nichts gsunderes ass a Taller Supp wenn, noch ebbs nochkummt."
There is nothing healthier than a bowl of soup as long as it is followed by something else.

Preparation: 5 minutes
Cooking: 20 minutes

6 slices sesame bread
2 tbs. butter

2 C. Riesling
2 C. chicken broth
1 small branch of rosemary
Pinch of sugar
4 egg yolks
1/2 C. cream
1/2 tsp. cinnamon
1/8 tsp. pepper
1/4 tsp. nutmeg

1. Butter the sesame bread and bake in oven at 325°F until golden and crispy. Set aside for garnish.
2. Simmer Riesling, chicken broth, rosemary, and sugar over low heat in a covered pot for 20 minutes.
3. Mix egg yolks and cream in bowl. Pour the soup in while whisking. Return the soup and egg yolk mixture to the pot. Add cinnamon, pepper, and nutmeg, and whisk over low heat until the soup thickens slightly.
4. Remove the rosemary and ladle into bowls. Garnish with croutons and fresh rosemary and serve.

Tips and suggestions:
Any white wine and bread may be used here, but the flavor will change accordingly.
Pair this with a sweet white wine.

Rabbit with Dijon Mustard Sauce, Mashed Carrots and Potatoes,
Curried Endive Salad, Red Cabbage with Apples

Rabbit with Dijon Mustard Sauce

"Has met senft"

Lapin à la moutarde de Dijon

Preparation: 5 minutes
Cooking: 50 minutes

1 rabbit, cut in pieces
3/4 tsp. salt
3/4 tsp. pepper
3 tbs. Dijon mustard
1/4 C. butter
1 tbs. olive oil
1 large yellow onion, sliced
1 C. mushrooms de Paris, sliced
2 C. dry white wine
1/2 cube of chicken bouillon
1 tbs. parsley
1/2 tsp. herbes de Provence
1 tomato, chopped
1 tsp. crème fraîche (pg. X)

1. Rub the salt, pepper, and mustard onto the rabbit. Melt half of the butter with oil in a saucepan over high heat. Brown the rabbit pieces on all sides. Remove the rabbit and set aside.

2. Lower heat. Add the remaining butter to the pan and sauté the onions until transparent. Add the mushrooms; cover and continue to sauté until the onions are golden.

3. Add the wine, bouillon, parsley, herbs de Provence, tomato, and the browned rabbit pieces. Cover and simmer for 40 minutes.

4. When the rabbit is done, remove from heat and stir in crème fraiche. Serve.

Tips and suggestions:
The liver may be sautéed with the rabbit to add flavor. Remove it early on so that is doesn't toughen.

Curried Endive Salad with Apples

"Andiji salad met Äpfel un Curry"
Salade d'endives aux pommes et curry

Endive is a pleasantly bitter lettuce that is popular in Europe but more difficult to find in the US.

Preparation time: 5 minutes

4 endives
1/2 C. curry vinaigrette (see recipe)
2 golden apples
1/2 tsp. sugar
Pinch of curry

1. Cut endives in half lengthwise and remove core. Slice endive leaves into thin strips. In a bowl, toss with half of the vinaigrette.

2. Peel, core, and slice apples. Mix with other half of the vinaigrette.

3. Pile the endives in the middle of the serving platter. Surround endives with apples. Sprinkle the curry powder and sugar over the apples and serve.

Tips and suggestions:
This may be made a day ahead of time to allow the flavors to "marry."
Any sweet crispy apple may be substituted for the golden apples.
Purple onions, blue cheese, bacon, walnuts, and pears all go nicely with this salad.

Mashed Carrots and Potatoes

"Galorewe pureé met Grumbeere"

Purée de carrottes et pommes de terre

Preparation: 5 minutes
Cooking: 20 minutes.

2 large potatoes
5 C. carrots
2 tbs. butter
1 tbs. crème fraîche (see recipe)
1 cube chicken bouillon
1/2 tsp. salt
Pinch of pepper
Pinch of nutmeg

1. Peel and cube the carrots and potatoes. Boil water with cube of chicken bouillon and a pinch of salt. Add potatoes and carrots and boil for 15 to 20 minutes until a fork pierces them easily. Strain.
2. Add butter, salt, pepper, and nutmeg, and mash with the carrots and potatoes. Leave a few small chunks for texture.

Red Cabbage with Apples

"Rotkrüt mit Aepfel"

Chou rouge aux pommes

Preparation: 10 minutes
Cooking: 40 minutes

1 head red cabbage
1 liter water
1 cube chicken bouillon
2 golden apples
3 tbs. sugar
1/2 bottle red wine
Salt to taste

1. Quarter the cabbage and remove the core. Slice the cabbage leaves thinly.
2. Boil water with bouillon cube. Add cabbage, whole apples, sugar, and wine. Reduce heat, cover and simmer for 30 to 40 minutes until most of the liquid is gone. Be sure to stir occasionally.
3. Peel, slice, and core the apples and toss with cabbage. Salt to taste. Serve warm.

Some variations include adding the following:

1 tsp. of curry
Whole roasted chestnuts
Onions and clove

Caramelized Pears

Poires caramélisées

Preparation: 5 minutes

Cooking: 15 minutes

3 pears
1 vanilla been
1 tsp. butter
2 tbs. raisins
2 Tbs. sugar
1 tbs. honey and herb vinegar
Pinch salt
Pinch of "4 spices"
1/2 C. white wine
1/2 C. roasted hazelnuts

1. Peel, core, and slice the pears. Slice the vanilla been in half.
2. Melt butter in a saucepan and sauté the pears and raisins over high heat until they start to color.
3. Lower the temperature and add sugar, vinegar, salt, vanilla bean, 4 spices, and wine to the saucepan. Simmer until the liquid thickens into a sauce. Remove from heat. (If the pears start to get too soft, remove and continue to simmer the liquid and raisins until the sauce is finished.)

Tips and suggestions:
Walnuts, pecans, pine nuts or almonds may be used to replace the hazelnuts.
Leftover schnapps marinade may be added to the wine in this recipe.
Champagne vinegar or white wine vinegar may be used to replace the honey and herb vinegar.
One tsp. of vanilla extract may be used to replace the vanilla bean.

Alsatian Cheese Tart

"Bibeleskäs Kueche"

Tarte au fromage blanc

Preparation: 20 minutes

Marinade: 8 hours

Baking: 40 minutes

1/2 C golden raisins

1/4 C. pear schnapps

1 short crust pastry (pg. X)

1/2 C. sugar

4 egg yolks

2 tsp. cornstarch

1 tsp. vanilla extract

1 tbs. lemon zest

1/3 C. cream

1/3 C. crème fraîche

2 C. fromage blanc

4 egg whites

1/2 tsp. vinegar

2 tbs. powdered sugar

Butter and flour to prepare the baking dish

1. Marinate the raisins in the schnapps overnight.
2. Preheat oven to 425°F. Butter and flour a round cake pan and line with the short crust pastry. Cover pastry with wax paper and fill with dry beans to keep the shape of the crust stable. Prebake the crust for 15 minutes until it starts to color. Remove from the oven and cool. Lower the oven temperature to 375°F.
3. Mix the sugar and egg yolks until they turn a light yellow. Mix in the starch, vanilla extract, and lemon zest. Mix in the cream, crème fraîche, and fromage blanc.
4. Drain the raisins and set aside the liquid. Spread the raisins over the cooled pastry crust.
5. Beat the egg whites with the vinegar until they form stiff peaks. Gently fold into the fromage blanc mixture until you have a uniform batter. Pour the batter over the raisins.
6. Bake for 30 to 40 minutes until the top is golden brown and the center is still slightly soft. Remove from oven and cool.
7. Sprinkle the tart with the powdered sugar and garnish with roasted hazelnuts, raisins, and pears.

Tips and suggestions:

Any eau-de-vie or brandy may replace the pear schnapps. You can use cream cheese for this, but lower the amount to 1½ C. and add 1/2 C. of cream. Add another egg to obtain a lighter texture.

Ricotta may also replace the fromage blanc. Lemon zest may be replaced with 1 tsp. of lemon oil.

Raspberries or strawberries may replace the pears and raisins.

Temps de Noel

December

Foie Gras Pâté with Truffles and Cranberries

Scallops with Late Harvest Wine Sauce

Sorbet and Schnapps Pause

Roasted Guinea Hen with Bacon and Prunes

Fresh Cheese Dumplings

Green Beans

Mixed Lettuce Salad with Cinnamon Vinaigrette

Fruit and Cheese Platter

Glazed Chestnuts

Chestnut Butter Cream

Yule Log Chestnut Cake

Spiced Breads

Aniseed Cookies

Wine Suggestions
Appetizers—Pinot Gris Late Harvest Wine
Meal—Morgon or Pinot Noir
Dessert—Mulled Orange Wine or Pinot Gris Late Harvest Wine

Mother Christmas

"Geteilti Freid isch doppelti Freid, geteilts Leid isch halbs Leid."
Shared joy is double the joy, shared pain is half the pain!

Christmas is a special time for families around the world and Alsace is no different. The ambiance in cities around the region is much enhanced by the presence of numerous "Marchés de Noël" (Christmas markets), which are open-air markets composed of lines of little wooden kiosks kept by artisans and merchants selling cakes, crêpes, spiced breads, ornaments, and anything else one might want for celebrating Christmas. Closely spaced stands sell vin chaud (mulled wine) so that passersby can keep themselves warm. Cities are adorned with lights and decorations on every street. Strasbourg titles itself the "Christmas capital" of the world and nearby rival Sélestat claims to have decorated the first Christmas tree during an eighth century visit to the city by Charlemagne. The celebrations start December 6, St. Nicolas' Day, and continue through to the New Year. Tourists from all over Europe and Alsatian Christmas shoppers wander about the streets of Strasbourg, enjoying the splendid sounds and scents, filling the while buying presents and goods from the kiosks.

When I first started to put down on paper the various stories from Ben's life for our cookbook, it was clear that December would be the most special month of the year. Ben requested that we dedicate this month to his mother. After all, it is often our mothers who inspire our deepest affection. Here is a Christmas memory that Ben recounted to me one evening shortly after Christmas.

"Every day at our house, my mother placed a plate on the table for the poor. It was there for anyone who might stop by." Ben paused. "My mother took in those who were in need just like she took me in. If it was cold outside, it was always warm in our home." Ben was lost in his memories as he spoke of his mother. When Ben was seven years old, a classmate asked him if he had written his letter to Père Noël (Santa Claus) yet. Ben responded, "No, my mother takes care of that for me." The young classmate replied bluntly, "That's not your mother; she only takes care of you." At once, Ben was filled with sadness and anger. He didn't answer the boy; he only turned and ran home. Seeing him enter the house, his mother asked him why he was crying. Ben said that it was nothing, that there were snowflakes in his eyes and that he didn't cry. He hurried to his room and wept with all his heart. His eyes were all red and swollen. He was surely the most unfortunate person in the whole world. His mother came into the room and took him in her arms and caressed his forehead. She had understood his sadness without his having to say anything. She always knew what was wrong. She knew everything. She explained that there are people in this world who enjoy making others suffer needlessly, but these aren't intelligent people. They are people without a heart, without love, but they must be the saddest people of all. She held him close and said, "Ben, you've been mine since you can remember and you will be mine until you remember no more." On Christmas day there were many presents under the tree. He kept trying to smile. But when they took a family photo, he hid behind his brother because he knew he wasn't one of them. After the gifts were opened, his mother had everyone sit together and said there was one last gift. Everyone seemed to know except him. She handed him a package that contained legal adoption papers giving him the family name. They took another picture in which he stood proudly beside his mother. Ben, being of Algerian descent, would experience difficulties from time to time as he lived the life of an Alsatian, spoke the local dialect, but still looked a little different anyway. Because of his mother, Ben learned to forgive these people. He also learned to have empathy and show kindness to strangers, and that is something that I can personally testify to. Today, Ben's mother is no longer here, and it is not the same, but life always changes. To honor her memory he continues the tradition of the family Christmas dinner, followed by mass, and a toast to her memory with a special bottle of wine. So it is in this spirit that we leave you with a menu that his mother loved to cook for the family Christmas dinner. We wish you a Merry Christmas, Happy Holidays, and bon appétit!

Tree Light

Foie Gras Pâté

"Genslewer pâté"

Pâté de foie gras de canard

The Romans brought with them the technique of fattening goose liver when they entered Alsatian territory in 58 BC. The result was highly appreciated and applied to ducks as well. It is symbolic of the winter holidays and can be served cold as in this recipe or lightly sautéed with apples and butter.

Preparation time: 20 minutes
Marinade: 24 hours
Baking: 45 minutes

1 lb. duck liver (foie gras)
2 black truffles (optional)
1 tbs. cognac
1/8 tsp. cinnamon
1/8 tsp. nutmeg
1/8 tsp. coriander
1/2 tsp. salt
1/2 tsp. pepper
2 pinches of saffron

6 pieces of toast
Fresh cranberries

Ceramic baking dish with lid

1. Peel the skin of the frois gras. Break into pieces gently with your hands and remove any large blood vessels. Place the frois gras pieces in glass bowl and marinate with the cognac, salt, pepper, cinnamon, coriander, saffron, and nutmeg for 24 hours.

2. Preheat the oven to 350°F.

3. Slice the black truffles thinly.

4. Take a covered ceramic baking dish and place half of the marinated duck liver inside. Layer the truffles in the center and cover with the rest of the duck liver and marinade. Cover with lid. Place ceramic bowl in a larger dish and pour warm water to cover half the terrine. Bake for 45 minutes.

5. Cool without uncovering and then place in refrigerator for 24 hours.

6. Serve with toast and fresh airelles.

Tips and suggestions:

This stays fresh for up to fifteen days in refrigerator.

To save money, use miettes de truffes, or the small broken pieces of truffles.

Scallops with Late Harvest Wine Sauce

"Jakobsmueschle met Spetherbscht"
Coquilles Saint-Jacques au vendage tardives

Preparation: 5 minutes
Cooking: 15 minutes
Baking: 10 minutes

6 empty scallop shells
6 large scallops
6 fresh mussels
3/4 C. late harvest white wine
1/4 tsp. salt
1/4 tsp. pepper
1 shallot, minced or pureed
1 tbs. butter
1/2 tsp. flour
1 tsp. parsley
1/4 tsp. nutmeg
2 tbs. crème fraîche (pg. X)
1/4 C. Paris mushrooms, sliced
1/2 C. popcorn shrimp, peeled and deveined
1 tbs. capers
1 lemon, sliced into wedges

1. Place the scallops and mussels in a small saucepan. Add 1/2 C. of the wine, salt, and pepper. Simmer for 5 to 10 minutes over low heat until the mussels open. Remove the seafood and set aside. Remove the mussels from their shells.

2. In a saucepan sauté the shallots in the butter until transparent. Stir in flour. Don't let it brown. Add the wine left over from the seafood. Simmer over low heat for 2 minutes while stirring until sauce thickens. Remove from heat and stir in parsley, nutmeg, and crème fraiche.

3. Place the empty shells on a baking tray and fill each one with 1 tbs. of the sauce. Arrange 3 slices of mushroom on the side of each shell. Place a scallop and mussel in each and top with shrimp and capers.

4. Stir in 1/4 C. of late harvest wine to the remaining sauce. Pour 1 tbs. of this over the seafood in each shell. Bake in oven for 10 minutes at 325°F.

5. Serve hot with wedges of lemon and a glass of late harvest wine.

Tips and suggestions:
This may be baked in ramekins instead of shells.

Sorbet and Schnapps Pause

"Elsässicher sorbet met schnaps"
Trou Alsacien

This is a digestive that burns away the fat and cleans the palate.

Preparation: 5 minutes

6 scoops yogurt sorbet
3/4 C. Marc de Gewustraminer

1. Place a small scoop of sorbet in each bowl and pour 2 tablespoons of schnapps over each.

2. Serve as a digestive between two dishes.

Tips and suggestions:
Lemon sorbet may be substituted for the yogurt sorbet.
Any eau-de-vie or grappa may be used to replace the Marc de Gewustraminer.

Roasted Guinea Hen with Bacon and Prunes

"Perlhehner met Speck"

Pintarde bardée de lard aux pruneaux

Preparation: 20 minutes
Baking: 50 minutes

Stuffing:
2 tbs. whole milk
2 cloves
1 yellow onion, diced
2 cloves garlic, minced
2 tbs. parsley
1/2 tsp. tarragon
1/4 tsp. coriander
1/8 tsp. saffron
2 black truffles, sliced (optional)
1/8 tsp. powdered mustard
1 tbs. duck fat
1/4 tsp. balsamic vinegar
1/4 tsp. salt
1/2 tsp. pepper
3 egg yolks
1/4 tsp. pine honey
1/2 apple, diced
1/4 C. veal kidneys or liver, minced (optional)
1 tsp. Cointreau liqour (optional)
1/8 tsp. nutmeg
1 tsp. butter
1/2 C. dry bread

1 guinea hen, gutted
6 strips of bacon
12 prunes
2 tbs. butter
1/2 tbs. duck fat
1/2 C. Bordeaux

1. Preheat oven to 350°F.
2. Warm milk over low heat with 2 cloves for 5 minutes and cool. Remove cloves.
3. In a large mixing bowl mix onion, garlic, parsley, tarragon, coriander, saffron, truffle, mustard, 1/2 tbs. duck fat, balsamic vinegar, clove infused milk, salt, pepper, egg yolks, and honey.
4. Peel and dice the apple. Sauté apple with kidneys, Cointreau, nutmeg, and 1 tsp. of butter over low heat for 15 minutes. Cool and add to the stuffing.
5. Chop bread into small pieces and add to the stuffing.
6. Fill the guinea hen with the stuffing and close. Crisscross 2 strips of bacon over the opening and lay the other 4 across the top of the guinea hen.
7. Butter a roasting pan with 2 tbs. of butter and place the hen inside. Brush 1 tbs. of duck fat over the hen. Place the prunes in the pan around the hen.
8. Bake for 50 minutes. After 15 minutes pour the Bordeaux over the hen and baste occasionally until finished cooking.

Tips and suggestions:
Chicken, duck, or turkey may be used to replace the Pintarde (guinea-hen).
Small broken pieces of truffles may be used to save money.

Fresh Cheese Dumplings

"Kaesknepfle"

Quenelles au fromage blanc

These "globi" as the Romans called them arrived in Alsace over two thousand years ago. The Romans brought them to Alsace, where families handed down the recipe from generation to generation.

Preparation: 15 minutes

Repose: 1 hour

Cooking time: 10 minutes

1 C. fromage blanc

1/4 tsp. salt

Pinch pepper

Pinch nutmeg

3 eggs

1 C. flour

1 tbs. butter

1 tbs. crème fraîche (pg. x)

1. Strain the fromage blanc in a cheesecloth for 1 hour.
2. Place the strained cheese in a large bowl and add salt, pepper, nutmeg, and eggs. Mix well. Add the flour. Mix until you have a smooth thick paste. Cover with a cloth and let rest for 15 minutes.
3. Bring a large casserole of water to a simmer. Dip 2 spoons into the boiling water and then use the spoons to form a dumpling from the batter. Gently drop the dumpling into the simmering water. Take care to give the dumplings plenty of room at first so they don't stick together.
4. Let the dumplings poach for 10 minutes until they rise to the surface and double in size. Strain.
5. Before serving, sauté the dumplings in butter until they start to color. Add crème fraîche and serve warm.

Tips and suggestions:

There are many variations to this from family to family, such as the addition of cubed bacon, chives, or chervil.

Green Beans

"Greni Bohne"
Haricots verts

Cooking: 15 minutes

1 cube of chicken bouillon
1 lb. green beans, fresh
Ice water
1/2 tbs. butter
1/2 shallot, minced
1/8 tsp. salt
1/4 tsp. parsley

1. Boil water with chicken bouillon cube. Add green beans and cook for 10 minutes. Remove green beans and place in ice water quickly to stop the cooking.
2. Heat butter in saucepan over high heat and sauté shallots with salt for 1 minute. Add beans and parsley and sauté for another 2 to 3 minutes. Make sure that the beans stay a little crisp.

Tips and suggestions:
The shallots may be replaced with garlic or lemon.

Mixed Lettuce Salad with Cinnamon Vinaigrette

"Gegruselter salad"
Salade mixte

Preparation: 5 minutes

1/2 C. nutmeg vinaigrette (see recipe)
1/8 tsp. cinnamon
1 bowl of mixed lettuce

1. Whisk cinnamon into the vinaigrette.
2. Toss with salad in a serving bowl.

Tips and suggestions:
You may use balsamic vinaigrette in place of the nutmeg vinaigrette.

Fruit and Cheese Platter

"Olst un e Blateau Käs"
Fruits et plateau de fromages

Preparation: 5 minutes

1. Arrange slices of bread, fruit, nuts, and cheese on platter.

Cumin bread
Rye bread
Chevre Valençay
Munster
Contee
Emmental
Roqeufort
Crottin de chavignol (goat cheese)
Mimolette
Camembert rustic
Mont d'Or
Brie
Butter
Pear, sliced
Red grapes
White grapes
Walnuts

Tips and suggestions:

This is meant to serve after the guinea hen and before the dessert. Any variety of cheeses, fruit, and bread may be used according to taste and availability. Some possible substitutions include the following:

Cheddar—Mimolette   Blue cheese—Roquefort   Swiss cheese—Emmental

You may serve this with red, white, or hot mulled wine.

Spiced Breads

"Lebkueche"

Pain d'épices

Since the sixteenth century, spices such as cloves, cinnamon, and cardamom have made their way from the Orient into Alsace. Each family soon developed their own recipe for spiced breads that were handed down from generation to generation. The recipes hold a source of family pride. Gatherings of village women presenting their various recipes have been recorded as early as 1586.

Advance Preparation: 1 week
Preparation: 10 minutes
Baking: 20 minutes

1 egg
1/4 C. honey
1/2 C. brown sugar
1/2 C. candied lemon peel
3/4 C. candied orange peel
1 C. chopped walnuts
1/2 C. diced candied ginger
1/3 C. butter
1/3 C. orange juice
1 tbs. lemon juice
1 C. rye flour
1 C. wheat flour
4 tsp. baking powder
3 tbs. cinnamon
1 tsp. cloves
1 tsp. ground fennel
1 tsp. nutmeg
1 tsp. ginger
2 tsp. star anise
1/2 tsp. salt
1/2 tsp. pepper

Glaze:
1 C. powdered sugar
3 tbs. lemon juice
1 tbs. schnapps or brandy

1. Preheat oven to 300°F. Butter and sugar a shallow baking sheet.

2. Whisk egg with honey and brown sugar. Stir in the lemon and orange peels, walnuts, and candied ginger. Melt butter and stir into orange juice and lemon juice. Stir into the egg mixture.

3. Sift together the dry ingredients and stir into the egg mixture with a wooden spoon. Mix by hand for 5 minutes, then let stand for 15 minutes.

4. Spread batter onto the baking sheet to the thickness of about 1 inch. Bake in oven for 1 hour. Cover with wax paper if the top starts to burn.

5. Cool and remove from tray.

6. Prepare the glaze. Mix powdered sugar, lemon juice and schnapps. Drizzle over the spiced bread. Cut into small squares and discard the edges. Serve with mulled wine.

Tips and suggestions:
Some variations include the following:

Almonds or hazelnuts in place of the walnuts

No fruit, nuts, ginger, or citrus peels at all

Wheat flour only

Yule Log Chestnut Cake, Spiced Breads, Aniseed Cookies, Glazed Chestnuts

Yule Log Chestnut Cake

"e Baümküeche"

Bûche de Noël

The burning of the Yule log comes from an ancient Scandinavian tradition celebrating the winter solstice. Originally, a trunk of a tree was cut down and dragged to the house with great ceremony. There it was kindled with holly, sprinkled with mulled wine, and burned in the hearth all night in order to burn away the trouble of the past year and bring good luck for the coming year. The tradition spread through England, France, and Italy, and eventually became a Christmas tradition until family hearths began to disappear. At that time, people improvised by using a smaller log with candles as a table centerpiece. Eventually this too was replaced by the cake we have today.

Preparation: 30 minutes
Baking: 10 minutes.
Refrigeration: 20 minutes

Sponge cake:
1 tbs. butter
Wax paper
8 egg yolks
1⅓ C. sugar
1 tsp. brandy
1 tsp. vanilla
1 tsp. cornstarch
1/3 C. chestnut flour
2/3 C. wheat flour
8 egg whites
1 tsp. vinegar

To decorate :
1 tbs. brandy
2 tbs. cooking syrup from glazed chestnuts
2 tbs. crème fraîche (pg. X)
1/4 C. chestnut cream
Chestnut butter cream (pg. x)
1 C. glazed chestnuts (pg. x)
1/2 C. chopped dark chocolate
1 tsp. cocoa powder

1. Prepare the sponge cake. Preheat oven to 375°F. Line a large rectangular baking tray with wax paper and butter well.

2. Beat the egg yolks with 1 cup of sugar until they turn light yellow and creamy. Add brandy, vanilla, and cornstarch. Mix well. Stir in the chestnut and wheat flours gently.

3. In another bowl, whisk the egg whites and vinegar until they form still peaks, adding 1/3 cup of sugar halfway through. Gently fold the egg whites into the batter half at a time.

4. Pour batter on the baking sheet. It should be about 1/2 inch thick. Bake in oven for 10 minutes until golden. Poke with a knife; if it comes out dry, the cake is done. Remove the cake from the oven and transfer it with the wax paper onto a slightly damp towel. Loosely roll the cake into a log shape. Let cool for 5 minutes and unroll.

5. Decorate the cake. Mix 1 tablespoon of brandy with cooking syrup from the glazed chestnuts and brush over the cake to moisten it. Mix the crème fraîche with the chestnut cream and spread a layer over the cake. Take 1/2 C. of the butter cream and spread a layer on top of the chestnut cream. Sprinkle 1/2 cup of chopped glazed chestnuts and 1/4 cup of chopped dark chocolate over the cake and then gently roll back into a log shape while removing the wax paper this time. Cut 1/4 of the cake roll at an angle and place the two pieces on a serving platter in the form of a tree branch.

6. Ice the cake with the rest of the butter cream. Dip the end of a wine bottle cork into the cocoa powder and press into the frosting to simulate knots in the wood then drag a fork to make markings like tree bark. Sprinkle with the rest of the chopped dark chocolate and decorate with whole glazed chestnuts.

7. Cool cake in the refrigerator for 20 minutes. Before serving, sprinkle powdered sugar over one side of the cake to simulate snow.

Tips and suggestions:
Other ideas for decoration: Dip pine leaves, basil, or rosemary into egg whites and water, and then sprinkle with sugar. Marzipan mushrooms or baked meringue to simulate mushrooms, crushed pistachios to simulate moss, cranberries to simulate holly.
Instead of burning the wine bottle cork, simply dip it in cocoa powder to simulate a knot in the bark.
You may replace the chestnuts with cherries, almonds, apricots, or candied fruit, using a corresponding jam in place of the chestnut cream.

Glazed Chestnuts

Marrons glacés

Nuts take on a symbolism at Christmas time in Alsace. Their hard shell and soft interior represent the human nature that hides the divine nature within.

"Wer de Karne asse will muess oi d'Nuss knacke!"
He who wants to eat the nut must break the shell!

Preparation: 5 minutes
Baking: 40 minutes

1 lb. peeled chestnuts
1 tbs. brandy
1 C. sugar
1 C. corn syrup
2/3 C. water
Vanilla bean

1. Place chestnuts and vanilla bean in a saucepan and cover with water. Simmer until tender. Drain, cool, and set aside.

2. Heat sugar, corn syrup, and 2/3 C. water in the saucepan until the sugar is dissolved. Stir occasionally. Increase heat and bring to a boil. Add the nuts. Save the vanilla bean until later. As soon as it returns to a boil, remove from heat, cover, and leave overnight.

3. The next day, uncover the nuts and bring back to a boil. Remove from the heat, cover, and leave overnight.

4. Repeat step 3 the next day, again adding the vanilla bean this time.

5. Add the brandy and store in sealed canning jars. After 2 to 4 weeks, drain the chestnuts and let them dry before using. The syrup may be reserved and used for pancakes or crepes.

Chestnut Butter Cream

"Crème de beurre de châtaigne"

Preparation: 20 minutes

1 C. butter, room temperature
1½ C. powdered sugar
3 egg yolks
1/2 tbs. vanilla
2 tbs. brandy
1/2 tbs. espresso
Pinch cinnamon
1/2 tbs. cocoa powder
3 egg whites, room temperature
1/4 tsp. vinegar
1/4 C. hot corn syrup
1/4 C. chestnut cream or puree

1. Make the glazed chestnuts and save the cooking syrup.

2. In a large bowl, cream butter and 1 cup of powdered sugar until light and fluffy. Keep cool in refrigerator.

3. Whisk egg yolks with 1/2 cup powdered sugar, vanilla, and brandy until creamy. Heat espresso and cinnamon for 1 minute over high heat. Slowly add to the egg yolks while whisking. Cool and stir into the cold butter cream along with cocoa powder and chestnut cream.

4. In another bowl whip egg whites with vinegar until they form soft peaks. While whisking, slowly add 1/4 cup of the hot corn syrup. Continue to whisk until the egg whites form stiff peaks. Fold the egg whites half at a time into the egg yolk cream gently. Place in refrigerator until needed.

Tips and suggestions:
Organic eggs are best for this recipe.
Use the hot syrup from the glazed chestnuts in place of the hot corn syrup.
Chestnut cream may be called crème de marrons in the store.

Aniseed Cookies

"Anisbredle"
Petits fours à l'anis

Preparation: 10 minutes

Refrigeration: 8 hours

Baking: 20 minutes

3 eggs

1 C. sugar

2 C. flour

1 tsp. whole aniseed

1. Butter and flour a cookie sheet.
2. Whisk the eggs and sugar until creamy. Stir in the aniseed. Gently stir in the flour until you have a smooth dough.
3. Form small cookies using two teaspoons and place on the cookie sheet.
4. Store in refrigerator over night.
5. Preheat oven to 350°F. Bake cookies for 15 to 20 minutes until the cookies rise. Do not let them brown on the top.

Tips and suggestions:

For a nice effect, sprinkle with granulated sugar when the cookies are still warm.

Trois Fenetres

Parvis

The Scent of Earth

The history of gastronomy in Alsace is like a family photo album. Food is that important; it is almost revered. Perhaps they know that food doesn't just fill our bellies. It helps define our traditions and our memories, which define a big part of who we are. It tickles our senses with smells, tastes, and sights that stay with us. Smell is one of the most powerful of our senses; it is no wonder that it can instantly transport us back to a place or a time.

In the collection of stories told by Ben, there was one about his grandfather. Every year early in August, he would take Ben with him to go find fresh wild asparagus. They would carefully pluck them from the ground and take a basket home to prepare dinner. Ben said that when he cooks asparagus, he remembers the scent of the earth on his grandfather's old weathered hands.

It's Christmas again. Another year brings with it a book full of changes. I'm home now in Minneapolis. Frederic lives in Quebec, and Ben is in France fighting cancer. I'm not sure what another year will bring, but the year in Alsace brought friendships bound together by the contents in this book. I can picture the lights and sounds in Alsace; it was the most glorious expression of Christmas that I've ever seen.

I can still feel the start of my days in Alsace and the smell of morning dew as I walk to get the first croissants from the bakery around the corner. They are still warm in the bag as I take them home for Frederic and me. I can hear the sounds of restaurants that line the street as they begin opening for the day. Later on, the sounds of singing will be drifting into the apartment from the restaurant across the street. Surprisingly, the YMCA song was always a favorite for the tourists. If it's Saturday, after breakfast I'll be walking by the grand cathedral on my way to the Saturday farmer's market and visiting with the herb seller, who has become a familiar part of my week. I miss these times in my days. I miss meeting with friends over a Guinness at the local Irish pub or outside of town for a tart flambée in one of the old farmhouses. But most of all I miss hearing the early morning knock on my door and knowing that Ben was stopping by with a pot of coffee to start the day with a friendly visit.

Back in Minnesota, familiar smells are drifting through the house. I've made mulled wine and spiced bread for my family this Christmas, and the scents are mingling with those from my childhood. It is the beginning of a new tradition for me. My father says the wine is too strong, but he'll only drink dessert wine; my mother asks me to fill her glass again. My entire family and I gathered around the phone earlier today to sing Merry Christmas to Ben, and even though he didn't speak much English, the message was clear. He laughed throughout the musical rendition. I could picture his larger-than-life smile and cheer. I hope Ben receives his Christmas sugar cookies soon, and I look around the room at my family. I know that as always life changes; it is the traditions that keep people close to us, keep our memories like those we love, close.

Ben continues to leave an empty space at the dinner table, as is his family tradition, but there is a part of me still sitting at the table with Ben and laughing over a well-prepared meal.

Index

Page numbers appearing in italic type refer to pages that contain illustrations.

978-0-595-36505-0
0-595-36505-1

Made in the USA
Lexington, KY
13 January 2013